Elegant and Easy Rooms

Other books by Dylan Landis:

Designing for Small Homes
Checklist for Your New Baby
Your Health & Medical Workbook
Your Healthy Pregnancy Workbook
Your Healthy Child's Medical Workbook

Elegant and Easy Rooms

250 Trade Secrets for Decorating Your Home

DYLAN LANDIS
Drawings by David McGrievey

A DELL TRADE PAPERBACK

A DELL TRADE PAPERBACK
Published by
Dell Publishing
a division of
Bantam Doubleday Dell Publishing Group, Inc.
1540 Broadway
New York, New York 10036

Book design by Jeannine Ford and Susan Maksuta

Library of Congress Cataloging in Publication Data
Landis, Dylan, 1956–
Elegant and easy rooms : 250 trade secrets for decorating your home / Dylan Landis ; illustrated by David McGrievey.
p. cm.
ISBN 0-440-50774-X
1. Interior decoration—Handbooks, manuals, etc. I. Title.
NK2115.L34 1997
747—dc21 97-816
CIP

Printed in the United States of America

Published simultaneously in Canada

October 1997

10 9 8 7 6 5 4 3 2 1

FFG

For the wonderful women
in the design writers group

ACKNOWLEDGMENTS

Many people invested their talent and time in this book, and I am thrilled for the chance to thank them.

David McGrievey drew the entrancing illustrations, many of them carefully researched. He knew what every picture needed to look like, even when I didn't. Plus he was a dream to work with.

Neil Janovic of Janovic/Plaza Decorating Centers answered, over many months, an endless stream of questions on paint and wallcoverings, while Kenneth X. Charbonneau of Benjamin Moore helped me understand the nuances of color.

The Pearl Paint publicity staff—particularly Wendy Lindquist, Angelica Irizarry, and Aurelia Cuevas—cheerfully wrote long explanatory memos about the art and craft supplies that came up in my conversations with designers.

Marcia Sherrill of Kleinberg Sherrill in New York designed the dreamy lampshade illustrated on page 74. Goodman Charlton of Los Angeles designed the curvaceous standing lamp pictured on page 137 and the ottoman on page 148. And I first learned about ordering Depression-era photographs from the Library of Congress in an article by James A. Baggett in *American HomeStyle & Gardening.*

Rhoda Jaffin Murphy, Bo Niles, Carol Prisant, and Lisa Skolnik—much-published design writers and, happily, friends—and my mother, Erica Landis, a wonderful editor with a good eye for design, all probed various chapters for flaws and made superb suggestions.

Mary Ellen O'Neill, my editor at Dell Publishing, improved things even more with her incisive questions and her love of the subject.

Jan Gottlieb was always there with the best kind of support.

And Dominick Abel, my agent, keeps opening new doors—and watching my back. I hope he knows how grateful I am.

CONTENTS

Elegant and Easy Rooms

HOW (AND WHY) TO USE THIS BOOK

Your home does not have to be perfect. Perfection is boring. It also costs too much.

This is a different kind of decorating book—about a friendlier, more accessible way to design or simply upgrade the rooms you live in. It is a compendium of smart decorating and styling ideas, written for people who care deeply about their house or apartment but aren't sure how to work the magic they admire in those gorgeous design magazines.

This is a book about how to pull rooms together in small ways and large—whatever suits your budget and your mood. It's about having a living room that invites you in again and again, a bedroom that works as a personal retreat, a dining room (or dining corner, if you live in a small space) that induces people to linger after dinner.

It's about achieving an overall *look*, if you choose to take it far enough, that can entice your friends to peer around corners and ask, "Did you have help?"

The truth is, most of us could use a little help. Most of us, faced with our own houses and apartments, aren't even sure where to start. If all the furniture is roughly in place, how can you even tell what's missing, or what needs to get done first?

This book is full of starting places—hundreds of them, in bite-sized tips, techniques, and pointers. Every idea is workable, designer-tested, and able to harmonize with scores of other tips from other pages. All can move you toward the three ingredients of a terrific room: *confidence*, *polish*, and *style*.

Confidence is a room's announcement that you knew exactly what you were doing (even if you didn't) when you put it together.

It's the way pictures are assertively grouped rather than indecisively hung by themselves. It's the way furnishings relate to each other in spirit and scale (*not* in period perfection). A confident room probably has a high-quality, come-hither sofa because its owner knew where to invest, not just where to economize; and most important, you can tell right away what this person loves—rich pattern on pattern, perhaps, or a sanctuary of taupe and beige.

Yet it doesn't have to be perfect. A confident room is not so different from a stylish woman who puts together an economical wardrobe, investing in a few simple well-made basics and assembling the rest with flair, inventiveness, and a sure hand. In the end, you simply want your rooms to feel, as Min Hogg, the brilliant editor of Britain's *World of Interiors* magazine, puts it, "kind of right."

Polish is the sense that things are finished, and it usually comes down to details. In a polished room, the pillows have welting, the lampshades look custom made (even when they're not), and the doors are dressed in good hardware. Polish means that the reading light shines where you need it but doesn't glare, and that there's always a convenient spot to put down a drink.

If you collect things—books, vintage blue glass, photographs of old roses—polish means you have a place for everything, however artlessly casual it may appear.

Style is what makes the place yours. It's what gives you the nerve to paint the dining room teal or red. It's the way you mass twenty candlesticks on a mantel instead of the usual pair; or have a dinner-plate-sized monogram embroidered on a living-room pillow.

Style, like polish, can also come down to details. Style is having the nerve to place your love seat at an angle, knowing it will open up the room; it's having the imagination to sew chandelier crystals to your curtains so they catch the sun; it's having the flair to gang mirrors, or even empty antique frames, as if they were pictures on the wall.

Every design idea in this book has been distilled to a single tip or decorating recipe. One may hold the perfect yellow for your living room walls. A second will explain an excellent spot in any room for built-in bookshelves. A third will suggest a way to dress your windows for less, and a fourth will show how to make a tiny bedroom feel (and function) like a larger one.

You won't feel drawn to every idea, because everybody has different taste. But all of these tips have been used at some time, in someone's home, successfully. Some are classic. A few are admittedly quirky. All of them have worked.

Choose any handful of ideas from these pages that appeals to your sense of comfort, your eye for design, your budget, and your home. They *will* work together—because your taste, and your personality, will bring the same spirit to bear on every decorating decision you make.

WHAT IF I DON'T REALLY TRUST MY OWN TASTE?

Then spend a little time learning what you love and what you don't. It will help your rooms look more harmonious and increase your confidence.

There's actually a technique for this, one that many interior designers recommend to their clients:

Start keeping two files, one labeled "What I Love," the other "What I Hate." Amass a stack of good design magazines, and tear out pictures that move you strongly, one way or the other. Use Post-its to note the particular details—a curtain, perhaps, or the color of a wall—that you feel either make or break a room.

When the files are full, examine each for what its pictures have in common. Is one file stocked with traditional furnishings, the other with contemporary built-ins? Are you repeatedly drawn to rich colors, or do you prefer the serenity of neutral tones? Are there five examples of regally striped wallpaper in the "Love" file?

Observations like this will give you a sense of personal direction. For precisely this reason, many high-priced designers and architects will begin a project by poring over the client's picture files.

WHAT WILL IT COST, AND WHAT SHOULD I SPEND?

This depends on your budget, and your priorities. Some of the decorating recipes in this book require only time and labor, like gathering pictures into a handsome constellation on the wall. For $20 you might buy a pair of ready-made glass-and-clip frames to update a pair of botanical prints. For $100 you can buy a halogen torchère that will beautifully light up a dim room. For $200 you might find a battered four-poster bed at a tag sale, then spruce it up with $30 worth of sandpaper and paint. For $1,000 you can pay a New York City building superintendent to paint a two-bedroom apartment. It depends on what you want, what you can afford, and how creatively you can bridge the gap between them.

In my opinion—and you must form your own—any improvement that makes a major difference in your *daily* experience of home and that costs less than $2,000 can probably be considered an excellent value. But you can make elegant upgrades for one-tenth that amount, and less.

Two other factors to consider:

- When do you need the best? A 1930s chair can be recovered in plush new mohair—just like the original upholstery—at $110 a yard, or in velvet (at discount) at $20 a yard. Ask yourself how you'll feel in three or five years: Would you rather have bought the mohair at any price? Or will you be glad you bought the velvet and saved?
- Renters should not spend big money on things they must leave behind. Spend $1,000 on a vintage rug, not on refinishing the floor. Don't have shelving built in when you can buy antique bookshelves and take them with you. This may seem obvious, but in years of renting I could never resist building in that shelving or refinishing floors. For me, it was a compulsion. If you can save the money, do.

Finally, remember that many interior designers furnish their own homes more with ingenuity than with money. I know of one, Christopher Coleman, who is quite established in New York—yet he wallpapered his living room with brown kraft paper. It looks so Zen-like in its simplicity, you'd never guess how little it cost. In my book that's the best kind of decorating there is.

WHAT IF I STILL NEED HELP OR ADVICE?

Consider hiring a professional interior designer.

Most people don't know it, but you can hire a designer for just a few hours, either to get some advice or to have your home "restyled." If you find yourself stuck—unable to choreograph a good furniture arrangement, find a great sofa, or choose a paint color you love—try a brief consultation with a designer.

For more information on how this works and what it costs, see "Do You Need an Interior Designer?" Appendix A.

IS THERE A CATCH?

Absolutely, but don't let it stop you.

The catch is that designers don't work this way.

Designers start with a grand plan and a floor plan, and they end with the details. They have excellent reasons for this, especially on big-budget jobs, and plenty of other books can tell you how to begin at the beginning, starting with a neatly drawn floor plan that you measure out yourself.

After eleven years of design journalism, I wanted to write another kind of book, one that adapts itself to the way many of us prefer to decorate: affordably, often impulsively, sometimes nervously, and with spurts of inspiration.

I call this "decorating by intuition."

The *premise* of this book is that with a modest budget and some expert advice, you can create welcoming rooms that exude confidence, polish, and style.

The *promise* of this book is that if you try any five ideas from these pages, your home will look better or work better. It doesn't matter whether you live in a house or an apartment, whether you rent or own. Any five "recipes" in any combination will make a difference you can appreciate, every time you walk in the door.

Start with any chapter, open to any page. You'll find dozens of tips—tricks of the trade on paint and color, furniture, window treatments, problem rooms, and the best mail-order catalogs. Choose two or twenty, to be combined as you wish.

WHERE DO ALL THESE DECORATING IDEAS COME FROM?

Much of what I've learned has come from writing about the work of interior designers, and I am in awe of their talents.

A good designer knows how to draw up a budget, what to invest in, when to take shortcuts, how to avoid mistakes, how to work expertly with color, form, and proportion—and how to incorporate your taste throughout. If you find yourself unable to make a single decorating decision—a panicky state that *The New York Times* once called Decoraphobia—it may be time to hire a designer for some short-term help.

But it's also possible that you simply need more confidence, and some high-caliber ideas. That's what this book is for.

I suggest you keep a decorating log as you go—a notebook of

paint colors, fabrics, wallpapers, and window treatments. Tape swatches into the log; write down product names and numbers; save the names and addresses of carpenters, paperhangers, closet organizers, upholsterers, and anyone else who's worked on your rooms.

You might also designate a section for workers recommended by friends; you may not need a great plasterer now, but one day you may be glad for the reference. Have another section for critical measurements, like the length of the wall for which you hope to find a perfect console table, or the space between those two doorways in the hall. This section can be quite helpful at a flea market, should you find yourself wondering whether something will fit in the house.

Tip: *If you live in an apartment building, write down the measurements of the lobby door, elevator, and your own front door, which may restrict the size of your purchases.*

Finally, remember that a beautiful home is not frozen. Some people don't believe this—having paid a designer, they keep every vase where it "belongs"—but it's true. The best rooms evolve slowly. Paintings move from wall to shelf and back again. You decide to do something about the dining-room light, which is casting murky shadows. Perhaps you inherit a nineteenth-century writing desk. Or you decide to buy a new sofa. A year later you see a picture in *Metropolitan Home*, and decide that you can't sleep another night unless your bedroom is sage green and cream.

Our homes reflect us—and that makes them alive and ever-changing.

Savor the process. Like home itself, it can be full of joy.

CHAPTER ◆ 1

Paint and Color

Most people choose a paint color by poring over thousands of paint chips in the store and testing heaven knows how many, at $14 a quart, on their walls. But this chapter contains a narrower, more proven selection of colors that various interior designers swear by, or that I've personally seen and loved.

Does this mean you'll adore Mark Hampton's yellow or Alexandra Stoddard's blue? Not at all—but it means you're *potentially* saving time, money, and angst by trying a shade that a professional has tested, or that somewhere, in someone else's living room, looks gorgeous.

Three good guidelines on handling paint and color:

- If you love white walls, realize that white is actually a color, and use plenty of it. Order slipcovers in off-white, and stir in pale objects with plenty of textural contrast—some lustrous silk pillows, semisheer muslin curtains, a collection of vintage white McCoy pottery. Explore off-whites with character: buttercream, light taupe, or white with barely-there undertones of pink or gray. Make the white in your home look like a deliberate choice, not something done by default.
- Small rooms, or those with a sense of enclosure, practically beg for a backdrop of color. Among them: dining rooms, libraries, hallways, and foyers. In dining rooms, colored walls set the stage for candlelight and conversation; in libraries, they're contemplative in ways that white can rarely achieve. Hallways and foyers, often deprived of natural light, may look drab if painted white.
- Remember what the decorator Billy Baldwin said: No color you love is ever out of style.

MAKE YOUR OWN SWATCHES

Paint a piece of white paper with the color you've chosen for your walls, and take it with you when you shop for fabric or furnishings. It's the easiest way to find out if your selections will look harmonious.

DON'T CHOOSE PAINT FROM A PAINT CHIP

Instead, test the color where you plan to use it. Design magazines always point out that you can easily repaint if you don't like the first color you choose, but, in truth, painting is a production. Shelves must be emptied, furniture moved, floors protected with tarps, walls and moldings cleaned, and, in the end, everything restored to its previous position. You don't want to do it twice—or, far worse, talk yourself into living with a color you don't love.

Here's the professional way to test paint:

Start with white walls, as any other contrast will give you a false impression of the color you're testing. If the walls aren't white, apply a coat of primer, which is naturally white and which you will have to use anyway when you repaint.

Roll one large swatch—4 feet square, if possible—onto the darkest wall, typically the window wall, and another on the sunniest, typically the one opposite the windows.

Live with it a few days. If you aren't powerfully drawn to the color, try something else.

OIL PAINT OR LATEX?

Traditional designers use oil-based paint for a perfectly polished look. But unless you're working with one of them, you're better off with latex (water-based) paint. Latex costs less, smells less, is kinder to the environment, goes on more easily, dries in hours instead of days, and cleans up with soap and water.

FROM LOW GLOW TO HIGH SHINE

Latex paint comes in five finishes. Starting with the dullest, these are *flat* (almost completely matte; cannot be washed), *eggshell* (glows but doesn't shine), *satin* (a slight shine), *semigloss* (a definite gleam), and *high gloss* (shiny; stands up to scrubbing).

The usual prescription, followed by most paint professionals, is this: semigloss on the moldings, which may need to be scrubbed due to fingerprints now and then; and eggshell on the walls. You can't go wrong if you follow it.

VELVETY FLAT

Flat latex paint has a lovely soft finish that helps camouflage pits and pocks in old plaster walls, but as it can't be washed, it's always been wildly impractical. Now there's a flat latex paint you *can* scrub: Janovic's Armour Wall. It goes on and cleans up as easily as standard latex paint, comes in 1,600 colors, and can be computer-matched to a sample of paper or fabric. To order, call Janovic/Plaza—see "The Best Mail-Order Resources," Appendix B.

THE FIRST COAT

If you are painting your walls a color other than white, ask the paint store to tint the primer, or base coat, to nearly the same shade. (The paint store won't make them a perfect match, because you need to be able to see a difference between the part of a wall that's only been primed, and the part that's been primed *and* painted.) The tinting charge may run from $1 to $5 a gallon, depending on which pigments are called for, but you'll probably need one less coat of paint in the end.

A PALETTE OF WHITES

The perfect white room isn't monochromatic—it's a rich interplay of hues. Use one shade on walls, one on the ceiling, a third on the trim. The New Orleans design firm Holden & Dupuy, known for its crisp use of white, favors Linen White, China White, and Navajo White—all from Benjamin Moore, to be applied in any combination you choose.

A FAMILIAR WARMTH

The warm and familiar yellow-beige of a manila file folder makes a lovely, neutral wall color. C&J Katz, a Boston design consulting firm, found a perfect match in Benjamin Moore no. 141; they often use it in living rooms where they want warmth without strong color.

THE STONES OF PROVENCE

Jeanne-Aelia Desparmet-Hart, a French interior designer based in Larchmont, N.Y., likes to paint walls in pale stone hues that remind her of her native Provence. Her choices:

Walls—Benjamin Moore no. 976
Moldings—Benjamin Moore no. 977

THE WARMEST NEUTRAL

These colors will definitely register as neutral, but they'll give your walls a blush of color that's much warmer than pure white.

Benjamin Moore no. 127—has an undertone of palest peach
Pratt & Lambert's Italian Straw, no. 1752—extremely pale yellow
Pratt & Lambert's Moth Gray, no. 2140—a hint of taupe, like unbleached linen
Benjamin Moore HC-27—an exquisitely delicate beige

COMPARING OFF-WHITES

How do you choose between five shades of off-white? Cut up the strips of swatches you got at the paint store, and paste each swatch that you're considering onto a sheet of pure-white typing paper. You'll see the undertones of each color more clearly.

THE SOPHISTICATION OF SOFT GRAY

For a soft, almost dovelike gray, try Benjamin Moore no. 1550, a favorite of New York designer Nancy Klasen. She suggested it for a modern apartment I had in Chicago—with architectural features, like doors and columns, accented in a slightly darker gray (no. 1551), and trim and ceiling painted white (no. 967). The place felt sophisticated and serene.

CHAMELEON COLORS

For an element of subtlety and mystery, paint a room with a color that changes through the day as the light shifts. The following colors all have a multiple personality:

- Benjamin Moore HC-1, a historic sage green that ranges from delicate (in sunlight) to acidic (by lamplight). It's a favorite of C&J Katz. (For moldings, try Moore's White Dove, no. 06.)
- For a more muted green, suggests Donna Paul, author of *The Home Office Book* (Artisan), try Benjamin Moore HC-2.

- For a light sage green with yellowy undertones: Benjamin Moore HC-116. (Use Moore's Linen White on moldings.)
- For a pale peach that changes its tint through the day, try Benjamin Moore O-85.

A GENTLE WASH OF COLOR

A soft, dappled veil of color—ideal for disguising walls in bad condition—can be achieved by mixing latex paint with water until it becomes a translucent tint, then applying it in dabs or quick strokes with a natural sponge. But unless you enjoy the trial-and-error process of mixing, then testing, your own diluted color, consider some of the ready-made products at paint and decorating stores.

Two of the most common are Jocasta Innes's Colourwash Kits, sold exclusively at Pottery Barn stores, and French Wash One-Step Sponging Paint, found at paint and decorating stores. Both come in delicately faded hues—such as terra cotta, champagne, and light blue—that appear, thankfully, on the labels. There's no guesswork and no diluting; simply choose a color and sponge it on. And if you don't like the telltale marks left by the dab of a sea sponge, try making fast little C-shaped strokes instead, for a finish that French Wash calls "parchment."

FARMHOUSE WHITE

Scott Clark, a Long Island housepainter with an artist's eye, concocted his own antique white for a farmhouse renovation. His recipe: three parts Atrium White to one part Linen White, both from Benjamin Moore.

Tip: *Have the paint store make this up for you. They might charge a few extra dollars per gallon, but they have machines that can shake the paint vigorously until it's properly blended.*

AN ENGLISH-LIBRARY PALETTE

A traditional English library is marked by its aura of intimacy and its rich coloration. The walls may be paneled in mahogany, for example, or painted an almost Renaissance red. Mark Hampton, designer of highly traditional and beautiful rooms, draws on the following colors (all Benjamin Moore) for an English-library atmosphere that can transform any room in the house:

Warm venetian red, no. 1323
Dark forest green, HC-135
Buttery yellow, no. 311

Tip: *As a counterpoint for moldings, Hampton recommends either Benjamin Moore no. 932 or 925, both creamy off-whites. Choose whichever looks better to you.*

YES, BLACK

Confronted with a long, narrow, and sun-starved hallway in his own New York apartment, Mark Hampton painted the walls *black*, with crisp off-white moldings and ceiling. The effect is rich and sensual, like black velvet with white satin, and Hampton and his wife, Duane, adore it.

Tip: *This is one case where oil paint serves you better than latex, as black paint shows scuff marks and must be easy to clean. Hampton recommends a low-luster finish.*

IMPERIAL RED, ROYAL BLUE

Two deep luscious reds for the walls of dining rooms and other small spaces: Chinese Red by Sherwin-Williams, a color you might see on an Oriental lacquered tray; and Pratt & Lambert no. 1013, the rich dark red on my own dining-room walls.

For a deep oceanic blue, design writer and author Rhoda Murphy favors Martin Senour's Prophesy Blue.

SET ONE ROOM APART

Paint one room a rich color, and it will be vividly distinguished from all your other rooms—as if you had suddenly added on a small wing. Because your home now offers such different moods or experiences, it may end up feeling larger.

HISTORICAL COLORS

Paint colors in the eighteenth and nineteenth centuries were brighter, richer, and often darker than most people realize, for by the time we see them on antiques, they've had decades to fade. Some early American paint recipes have been recreated, however, by a historic-paint company called Stulb. If you feel good in traditional interiors, consider the colors and textures that go with them:

- Reproduction buttermilk paint, a collection from the Abby Aldrich Rockefeller Folk Art Center at Colonial Williamsburg. This water-soluble paint has a soft, almost powdery finish and comes in 14 historically correct colors, some with evocative names like Child's Rocker Bright Red and Dressing Table Blue. The manufacturer grinds its own natural pigments.

- Old Village paint colors. Twenty-three historic hues—some are warm, some earthy, some contemplative. Pearwood, a cross between olive green and taupe, is a dark neutral tone that could be lovely in a small hallway. Rittenhouse Red or British Red would be exciting yet traditional in a dining room, and Cupboard Blue could lend a sense of history to an inexpensive set of bookshelves.
- Reproduction whitewash. Gritty to the touch and white as snow, this whitewash is ideal for old walls with lots of blemishes, or too-new wallboard walls that could use some texture.

Bonus: Mention this book and Stulb will give you free color samples (regularly $3) and a 10 percent discount off 2 or more gallons of paint (regularly $39.95 a gallon). For color samples and information on all products, contact Stulb Co., P.O. Box 1030, Fort Washington, PA 19034-1030; tel. (800) 498-7687; fax (215) 654-1976.

PALE ROSE WALLS

Alexandra Stoddard, the New York designer and author, often paints bedrooms light pink; she says even her male clients find it a refreshing, relaxing color. The trick is to choose a pink that's clear and natural, not cloying or sweet. Her shade of choice—Fuller O'Brien's Beauty, no. C-23—is about the color of a peony.

COLORS THAT SING TOGETHER

You can enhance a room's character by including the ceiling and trim in your palette—whether you're using sunny hues or neutrals. The color marriages that follow are favorites of designer Barbara Southerland of Greenville, North Carolina, and New York City. (To find out which colors and combinations appeal to you, get paper swatches from the paint store and tape them down in groups on white typing paper.)

For a small room with punch:

Coral walls (Benjamin Moore no. 004)
Palest sky-blue ceiling (Benjamin Moore no. 844)
Clean white trim (Benjamin Moore's White Dove, no. 06)

For a dark sophisticated hallway:

Olive-green walls (Pratt & Lambert's Thyme, no. 1662)
Pale peach ceiling (Pratt & Lambert's Morrel, no. 1852)
Warm off-white trim (Pratt & Lambert's Ancestral, no. 1426)

For a sunny room anywhere in the house:

Lemony walls (Pratt & Lambert's Blonde, no. 1727)
Robin's-egg-blue ceiling (Pratt & Lambert's Big Sky, no. 1327)
Off-white trim (Pratt & Lambert's Linen, no. 1759)

For intense beach-house colors in a small foyer or powder room:

Hot, tropical coral walls (Pratt & Lambert's Azalea, no. 1868)
Restful sky-blue ceiling (Benjamin Moore no. 1639)
Warm off-white trim (Benjamin Moore no. 876)

PAINT AS A LONG-TERM INVESTMENT

Schreuder paint, made in Holland, is an oil-based elixir that yields a flat finish so matte, it looks like velvet. Schreuder paint turned up recently in a room by Ronald Bricke at the famous Kips Bay show house in New York. Visitors couldn't resist it; they kept breaking the don't-touch rules to stroke the elephant-colored walls.

A "Eurogallon" or 2.5-liter container of Schreuder paint costs $70, but it covers more space than an equal amount of American paint, being rich in pigment. You also shouldn't need to repaint for about ten years. This can be a terrific investment—*if* you own your own home, can afford to hire a professional painter (oil paint isn't a good do-it-yourself job), don't mind waiting days (rather than hours) for each coat to dry, and really crave a flawless backdrop.

To order swatches or paint, or to get the name of a retailer, contact Fine Paints of Europe at (800) 332-1556. The company also sells Martha Stewart paints in the same formulation; professional-size swatches are $15.

Tip: *If you've been stricken with a particular color from another manufacturer's line, Fine Paints of Europe will computer-match it at no extra cost.*

THE COLORS OF TRADITION

The real beauty of Ralph Lauren paint is not the designer label. It's the way the colors are organized into mistake-proof collections which have evocative names like Safari, Sport, and Thoroughbred. Any two or three or four shades from a single collection are designed to harmonize, so you can combine colors throughout the house without angst. You can also buy tools for special effects, to make walls look like suede, satin, or denim. Test them first on a small area to see if you're comfortable with the technique and happy with the results. Because the tools were created with amateurs in mind, these faux finishes, according to Lauren, qualify as do-it-yourself effects.

The paint is latex and costs less than some other big brands (about $21 a gallon). For names of stores that carry the paint, call (800) 379-7656.

THE PASSIONATE 1940S

Kenneth X. Charbonneau, a top color expert at Benjamin Moore, went back through the paint company's archives to find a color palette from the 1940s. If that is the era that speaks to you—with its orchid-printed barkcloth and rattan furnishings—here are the key colors, to be used in any combination. They're all Benjamin Moore.

Tea Rose—no. 053
Light Green—no. 550
Sunshine Yellow—no. 311 (incredibly warm on walls)
Wedgwood Blue—no. 1586
Oyster White, no. 956, or Ivory, no. 922

The passionate 1940s

PURE 1950S

This vintage paint palette, also from Benjamin Moore's archives, was popular in the 1950s. If you have fond memories of boomerang-patterned Formica, or if your coffee table and sofa are kidney-shaped, these may be your colors:

Turquoise—no. 670
Off White—no. 927
Sharon Rose, no. 024
Empire Gold—no. 201
Willow Green—no. 541
Forest Green—no. 602
Sandalwood—no. 1083

Tip: *Fifties colors run warm, so do include one of the greens for a cooling effect.*

EVOKE AN ITALIAN VILLA

If you've traveled to Italy, you've probably seen old villas and farmhouses with stucco walls. The color, usually ocher or terra cotta, is faintly mottled and aged by centuries of sun. Los Angeles interior designer D. J. Kami-Thompson came up with her own urban shortcut to this look:

Pure
1950s

Start with a clean white wall, lightly sanded and wiped free of dust. Don't bother patching or priming, as the finished look is supposed to be imperfect.

Buy latex paint in terra cotta. Choose either an eggshell finish or, for kitchens and bathrooms, semigloss. (Thompson also buys a small tube of universal tint in raw sienna, sold at paint stores for about $2, and stirs in a few drops to give the color complexity and depth. But this is optional.)

Wad up a few sheets of paper towels into a clump. Dab it, don't soak it, in the paint. Spray the toweling with a fine mist of water from a plant sprayer.

Now rub color on the wall in circles. Vary the pressure. Cover some areas more densely than others. Switch to new paper toweling as soon as the wad gets too soggy or tears. You may even want to go back over some areas after the wall dries, to make the coverage either more even or more stormy.

Not only will the room look distinctly Italian, but cracked or badly plastered walls will be well camouflaged by the technique.

Tip: *At the risk of sounding like a commercial, I suggest Bounty paper towels, as artists often use this brand for its absorbency.*

STRONG COLOR, JUST IN PASSING

Paint a hallway in your favorite color, without stopping to worry if it's a safe choice. Because hallways are transition spaces, not rooms for lingering in, you'll get to enjoy the color every day without having to soak in it.

THE GREEN DILEMMA

If you can't find the perfect shade of green for your walls, there's a reason: According to some artists, it's the hardest color to perfectly capture in paint. (I spent a week testing shades of apple green, never quite getting it right.) If in doubt, choose another color for the walls—and integrate green into your rooms through fabric, rugs, or accessories instead.

COLORS FOR STRONG SUNLIGHT

Wellborn paint, made in the Southwest, isn't sold in most states. But if you live in a hot sunny region of the country where vivid colors look magnificent, you may want to examine what Wellborn calls its "ultra-deep" hues—superintense purples, greens, and blues, all saturated with pigment. On request, the company will mail you free five-color strips (like the ones in your local paint store) in the color family of your choice, such as green or blue. Alternatively, for $15 plus $3 shipping, you can order a fan deck, a hinged collection of swatches showing a thousand Wellborn hues, including the 80 ultradeep shades. Finally, some stores in Texas, Colorado, and New Mexico carry the paint; ask the company for addresses.

Wellborn paint runs from $15 to $25 a gallon, with discounts for a 5-gallon batch. (Don't forget shipping; to New York City, for example, it would run about $24 for 4 gallons.) *Contact*: Wellborn-DE Corp., 215 Rossmoor Rd. S.W., Albuquerque, NM 87105; (800) 228-0883; in New Mexico (800) 432-4069.

Tip: *You can't return paint once it's opened, so before ordering, try to talk Wellborn into sending you a professional-sized, 3-by-5-inch chip of the color you've fallen in love with.*

MARTHA'S PAINT MARRIAGES

You need not be a Martha Stewart devotee to be utterly enamored with her new latex (water-based) paint. Every paint chip is keyed to a "combination card" bearing three more colors that coordinate with your original choice and with each other. In other words, fall in love with a single color, and Martha hands you the scheme for the entire room. All of the hues are drawn from nature—flowers, leaves, shells, the blue and green eggs laid by Martha's Araucana chickens, even the fur on her pets. The colors are subtle, but they glow. The paint is sold only at Kmart stores. For questions, call the toll-free hotline: (800) 627-8429.

KEEP THE TRIM CONSISTENT

If you change colors between rooms, whether slightly or dramatically, use the same shade of white on ceilings and trim throughout the house. Though the effect is subtle, it will keep all of the rooms related to each other. Two whites that go with virtually everything are Benjamin Moore's White Dove, and no. 967.

A CEILING OF BALMY SKY

A pale blue ceiling, implying the sky, makes an evocative "lid" in a room, regardless of its height. Alexandra Stoddard's choice: Fuller O'Brien's Fulcolor Atmosphere Blue.

SUNLIGHT OVERHEAD

A light yellow ceiling—just pale enough to stay in the background—can imply sunlight where none exists (or amplify it in a light-filled room). New York designer Thomas Jayne used this trick at the prestigious Kips Bay Boys and Girls Club Decorator Show House. His color choice: Benjamin Moore HC-4.

Or choose any breathy, atmospheric hue that you like. David H.

Mitchell, a Washington, D.C., designer, suggests only one rule: "Don't let that color have a relationship to anything else in the room, or it will pull the ceiling down." In other words, if your ceiling is a celery-mist color, don't use that shade of pale green in any of the furnishings or accessories.

THE PASTEL CEILING

Debra Blair, a New York designer, often paints her clients' ceilings either pale blue or lavender, evoking the sky. Her favorites:

Pratt & Lambert's Irish Mist, no. 1041 (a light amethyst color)
Pratt & Lambert's Cumulus, no. 1245 (extremely light blue)

THE POLISHED CEILING

If you are investing in a professional paint job, lavish some extra attention on the ceiling. Have it sanded to perfection, primed, and painted with semigloss or, if it's really in flawless condition (ask your painter), high-gloss white paint. The finish will help bounce light around the room and add a little gleam of its own.

Tip: *The kind of preparation needed for glossy paint is expensive, so lavish this on one key room where you entertain or spend a lot of time.*

HARMONIZING WALLS AND TRIM

If you are painting a room in a light or neutral color (for example, putty, taupe, or pale yellow), how will you know which white or off-white to use on the ceiling and trim? Washington, D.C., designer Barry Dixon uses this recipe:

For the moldings, mix one part of the wall color with three parts of pure white. (The paint store may agree to do this for you; if not, it can sell you inexpensive cardboard buckets that will make the mixing easier.)

For the ceiling, mix one part of the wall color with four parts of pure white.

"This assures you that all the tones will look good together," says Dixon. "An element of your wall color will shine through in everything else, and you are absolutely assured of having your room in harmony."

Tip: *To adjust for darker wall colors, increase the ratios in favor of white—use four parts of pure white for trim, five parts of pure white for ceilings.*

THE COORDINATED CEILING

A less ambitious recipe for relating the walls to the ceiling is to pour a cupful of your wall color into the white ceiling paint. (Use it on trim, too.) You'll barely perceive the tint, but it gentles the contrast slightly, making the room more of a seamless envelope.

PAINTED WOODWORK, NO GUILT

It seems like heresy to paint woodwork that someone has stripped back to its natural state. But if your dark wood trim injects a note of gloom in the room or simply looks insubstantial, remember that it may have been *designed* to be hidden under paint. Examine it closely: Is the grain gorgeous? Is the color rich? If not, it may be cheap wood that was never designed to show. (A carpenter can offer a second opinion.) By painting it white, you may be treating the woodwork as it was intended—and brightening a dark room, too.

TWO-TONE FURNITURE

When you paint a bureau, consider whether the piece might look more sophisticated if you combined two colors: one for the drawers, a second for the bureau frame. A line of coordinated spray paints makes this easy—both harmonizing the colors and applying the paint. The line is American Accents, made by Rust-Oleum, and its colors are grouped in collections (Classic, Garden, Tapestry, or Heritage). The shades in each collection are designed to work together.

Two-tone furniture

A GENTLE INTRODUCTION TO COLOR

If you are drawn to strong colors but fear they will overwhelm your walls, try this experiment: Paint two inexpensive chairs, or perhaps a small wooden table, the color of your dreams—sunflower, perhaps, or emerald. Live with it a week or two. It will help you decide whether you like strong color only in small doses or long to be more completely surrounded by it.

PLAN FOR TOUCH-UPS

Save some of your leftover paint in a glass jar with a tightly closed lid. The paint will stay fresh until it's needed for touching up scuff marks, and more important, the shade will be identical. (Different batches of paint may have very subtle differences in hue.)

***Tip:** Label the jars with the paint number or name. It's a good record to have should you need to repaint a whole room.*

CHAPTER 2

Walls

Many designers regard a blank wall as a canvas. Indeed it is—but paint is not your only medium. More types of wallcovering exist than most people realize. Some evoke faux finishes such as marbling; others are deeply embossed designs that survive from Victorian days.

Walls can also be quite expressive: Consider a few lines of poetry stenciled across a wall—or even a single wall coated with blackboard paint (the kind used on schoolroom chalkboards), allowing you to get whimsical with chalk and erase the "art" when you like. You probably don't want such special effects throughout the house, but they do let you turn a single room or just one wall into a personal or artistic statement.

The biggest mistake that many of us make with our walls is not overdecorating but *under*decorating. We roll on a coat of white paint not because we love white but because all the other options overwhelm us. Or, nervous about assertively wide stripes on wallpaper, we buy skinny ones that seem safe but end up making the room look dizzying.

The solution? Test-drive a few wall treatments before making up your mind. If you've fallen in love with a bold wallpaper design, buy a roll and tape it up. If you're drawn to the idea of writing on the walls, write on white paper first, and tape *that* up. Live with it for a few days or more. Ask a friend for an opinion. Then, as with all decorating decisions, follow your heart.

LARGE PATTERNS OR SMALL?

Contrary to what most people expect, a tiny wallpaper pattern won't make a small hall or powder room look airy. If anything, it visually shrinks the space. If you're drawn to an overscaled wallpaper design, such as cabbage roses, or a neoclassical design based on tall urns, find a small room in which to display it. Your eye will be tricked into perceiving a larger space.

THE VICTORIAN PRESSED-TIN EFFECT

In love with decoration for its own sake, the Victorians paneled their walls with elaborately embossed leather—until they came up with wallcoverings that emulated the look for less. These coverings are still made in all their original beauty; they often look like gorgeous faux plasterwork, or the fancy pressed tin that appears on Victorian ceilings. Among the decorating possibilities:

- Run a tall neoclassical frieze (essentially an oversize wallpaper border) of urns and swags all the way around the room, just under the crown molding. If your room has good proportions to start with, this will make it downright noble.
- Have the embossed covering applied only to the lower 36 or 40 inches of the wall. This section of the wall is called the dado. ("I call this decorating below the belt," the late designer Carleton Varney once wrote, "because that's exactly where a dado is—on the lower half of the wall.") You'll need to add

The Victorian pressed-tin effect

molding, or an embossed wallpaper border just above it, at chair-rail height, to separate the dado from the upper portion of the wall.

- Paper just the ceiling so it looks like fancy Victorian pressed tin—a lovely contrast to serene white walls.
- Paper just the walls (with no separate dado).

Among the coverings you'll find at better decorating and paint stores (or through the Janovic/Plaza catalog—see "The Best Mail-Order Resources," Appendix B) are Lincrusta, which feels like linoleum and was designed for dados; Anaglypta, a heavy cotton-fiber paper; and a newer embossed paper called Classic Coverup. All need to be painted once they're up.

PAPER-BAG TAN WALLS

New York interior designer Christopher Coleman walked into a paper supply store, bought a 500-foot roll of plain kraft paper about as wide as standard wallpaper, and applied it to his walls with wallpaper paste. It makes an evocative, neutral backdrop, and its matte finish hides imperfections in the plaster underneath.

Two Coleman tips:

- Buy only heavyweight kraft paper. (Ask for a grade of 70, which Coleman used, or even 80 or 90, which are heavier.)
- Overlap the edges one-eighth of an inch, rather than trying

to align them like standard wallpaper. This will keep the edges from lifting.

PICTURES AGAINST PATTERNS

When hanging pictures over wallpaper, use generously sized mats (a minimum of 3 to 4 inches wide) to separate the framed images from the patterned backdrop.

THE SOPHISTICATION OF STRIPES

A truly classic wallpaper pattern is a broad, tone-on-tone stripe—meaning that only one color is used. (Slight variations in hue or finish create the striped effect.) A stripe of about 4 inches wide is classic, whereas pencil-thin stripes, in some settings, may make your eyes swim.

For a room of subdued elegance, consider neutral stripes: white on white, taupe on taupe, the palest yellow on yellow, or soft gray on gray.

For a more European-looking or cozy feeling, try the same tone-on-tone stripe in a color that reminds you of an English library, such as hunter green, dark red, or tobacco.

Tip: *Flowers and stripes have been natural companions through years of decorating history, so when shopping for fabric to use in a striped room, consider florals.*

Bonus: *The vertical stripes will make your ceiling look higher.*

BUY THE BEST WALLPAPER (AND USE LESS)

The most beautiful paper is often handpainted or handprinted by artisans, or by old-guard companies like Scalamandre, Colfax & Fowler, Schumacher, or Brunschwig & Fils. The trick is to use it sparingly, where it will stand out—perhaps even more prominently than if you lavished it on all four walls. Among the possibilities:

- Paper the back wall of a niche.
- Paper the back panel of bookshelves.
- Paper the ceiling, as the Victorians did, and paint the walls with a color drawn from the wallcovering.
- Paper the wall only above chair-rail height; use paint below.
- Make tall, rectangular panels on the wall with picture molding or wallpaper borders, and paper inside the panels for a formal look. (To get the proportions right, experiment by taping up plain paper first.)

THE HANDPRINTED BORDER

Another way to incorporate handprinted or very expensive wallpaper is to use only a border. Run one band at chair-rail height

(36 inches from the floor) and another just below the crown molding.

THE UNEXPECTED BORDER

A designer in an online forum once explained how he ran a wallpaper border at the unusual height of 6 feet above the floor in a child's room. This would look just as intriguing elsewhere in the house, particularly in a room with no architectural distinction. Paint the top and the bottom portions of the wall differently, contrasting any two colors that please you. For subtlety, try two shades of a single soft color, such as sage, taupe, or light yellow. For drama, turn up the contrast, or use a color on the bottom and white on the upper portion and the ceiling. The variations are endless.

CUSTOMIZE A PAPER BORDER

Make a wallpaper border look richer and more prominent by snipping away the plain, solid-colored paper below the actual design. For example, if the border shows a twisted swag of fabric against a yellow background, use a straight-edge razor or scissors to remove the yellow paper just below the swag.

Customize
a paper border

CHALKBOARD ART

Blackboard paint, with its flat black finish, can turn all or part of a wall into an ever-changing contemporary artwork. Friends' doodles, snippets of poetry, caricatures, rough landscapes, marketing lists—all can be objects of artistic intrigue when plucked out of their usual context (the same idea that Andy Warhol applied to the Campbell's soup can).

Oil-based blackboard paint, the only kind, is carried at paint stores. Apply it over a fresh coat of primer using a foam or low-nap roller. To keep it looking seamless, always roll from a dry unpainted section of the wall into a wet, freshly painted section. The consistency of this oil-based paint should be like butter; if it "pulls" on the roller, thin it slightly with mineral spirits. Two coats should suffice.

The downside? It's a formidable job to repaint (though it certainly can be done, starting with primer) if you decide to go back to a white wall. An alternative is to buy a very large, ready-made blackboard and have it reframed in something carved or gilded.

Tip: *Keep chalk and erasers in a sculptural container on the coffee table. White chalk, rather than colored, is more evocative of old schoolrooms; keep this in mind if you want to evoke a vintage mood.*

Classic architecture

CLASSIC ARCHITECTURE

In a white-box room devoid of moldings and character, create a sense of architecture with wallpaper borders that are printed to resemble traditional plasterwork or woodwork. Look for something classic, like a Greek key, dentil, or egg-and-dart design; or a border of acanthus leaves.

THE ARTISTIC BORDER

An increasing number of wallpaper companies are producing borders that look more like handpainted art than like decoration—for example, a still life of fruit based on Baroque Dutch paintings, or an early American-style landscape with diminutive farmhouses and cows. The implication is that an itinerant painter stopped by your home about a century or so ago and painted this slender band of artwork on commission. Any home decorating store with a wide selection of wallcoverings should offer a good selection of borders.

LIVE WITHIN A POEM

Wall writing is the simple, expressive act of hand-lettering a line or two of poetry on the wall. The poetry can encircle the room like crown molding, just under the ceiling, or occupy part of one wall. You'll need alphabet stencils (sold at home decorating and art supply

Live within a poem

stores) in a handsome typeface and several sizes, so you can experiment; and the patience to figure out how much space each letter needs. Some typefaces come in a range of sizes, from less than an inch to a full 12 inches high, so look for a store with a good selection.

This is time-consuming but not hard. Stencil a few words onto plain paper and tape to the wall, experimenting until the size of the letters and the spacing between them looks right. Then calculate how many words fit nicely across the wall. Double-check, to avoid mistakes. With light pencil, outline the letters on the wall; it will help you place the stencils correctly.

The basic recipe: Hold a stencil in place with masking tape. Dab a stenciling brush (from an art or craft supply store) into the paint. Dab excess paint onto newsprint or paper toweling. Then "pounce" the brush over the surface of the stencil until you get the density of color you desire. Remove the stencil. Paint the letters in random order, so you're never working right next to a still-wet letter.

***Tip:** A book of quotations can be a source of inspiration; so can Shakespeare's sonnets.*

DOT, DOT, DOT

Van-Martin Rowe, a Pasadena, California, designer, has been known to stick round (dime-sized) dot stickers onto walls, either to surround a window with a border or to create a pattern above a chair rail. "They won't peel the paint," he says, "and you can take them off when you want. It's easy, and it's dramatic." The dots, by Avery, are sold in most stationery stores.

Rowe's tips: For subtlety, buy dots the same color as the wall; for a bit of giddiness, use a contrasting color. Stick them six to eight inches apart, and stagger the rows of dots bricklayer style.

RUBBER STAMPING

It doesn't get much easier than this: rubber stamps that make their stencillike marks on walls. Two good options for novices:

- Bookstores carry, or can order, the Stampability kits by Stewart and Sally Walton (Lorenz Books). The kits come with a 32-page book of instructions and three stamps, which vary depending on the theme you choose: Cherubs, Heraldic (includes a crown and fleur de lis), Folk Art, Hearts, Roses, Stars, Vineyard (with vine motifs), and Seashore.
- Complete kits, including three delicate shades of paint, are sold in Pottery Barn stores; the themes are ivy (with four stamps) and star, pear and grapevine (each with one stamp). Moisten the stamps with paint, using an artist's brush, and press; practice on paper first. If you buy the ivy stamps, you can paint tendrils of vine freehand to connect the leaves.

Tip: *You don't have to stamp an entire wall. Ivy, for example, looks best when spilling down from the top of a doorway or window, or growing all the way around the room at chair-rail height.*

PATTERNS WITHOUT PAPER

By stenciling a repeating pattern directly onto the wall, you can save the expense of buying and hanging wallpaper. You also get more control over the design—and if you ever want to change it, there's no paper to strip. Some sophisticated patterns now exist: eight-pointed starbursts, celestial suns and moons, pears, leaves, and many others.

Practice the spacing on paper first; then make small pencil marks on the wall where you want the designs to go.

Stencil catalogs are listed in "The Best Mail-Order Resources," Appendix B.

THE REPEATING ROLLER

In the 1940s painters sometimes used rollers into which a design had been incised; the pattern that resulted looked like a cross between wallpaper and old-fashioned block printing. An Italian company makes dozens of these rollers—some rather atomic, like 1950s boomerang designs, and some quite delicate, like fern and weeping willow. To print a wall in this fashion, you must be able to start at the top and reach the bottom—all in a straight line—without letting go of the roller. Go slowly, and practice first with a dry roller (of any kind) and a stepladder. This takes practice, but Janovic/Plaza, which sells the rollers by mail, swears it's a do-it-yourself project. See "The Best Mail-Order Resources," Appendix B.

Chapter ◆ 3

Windows

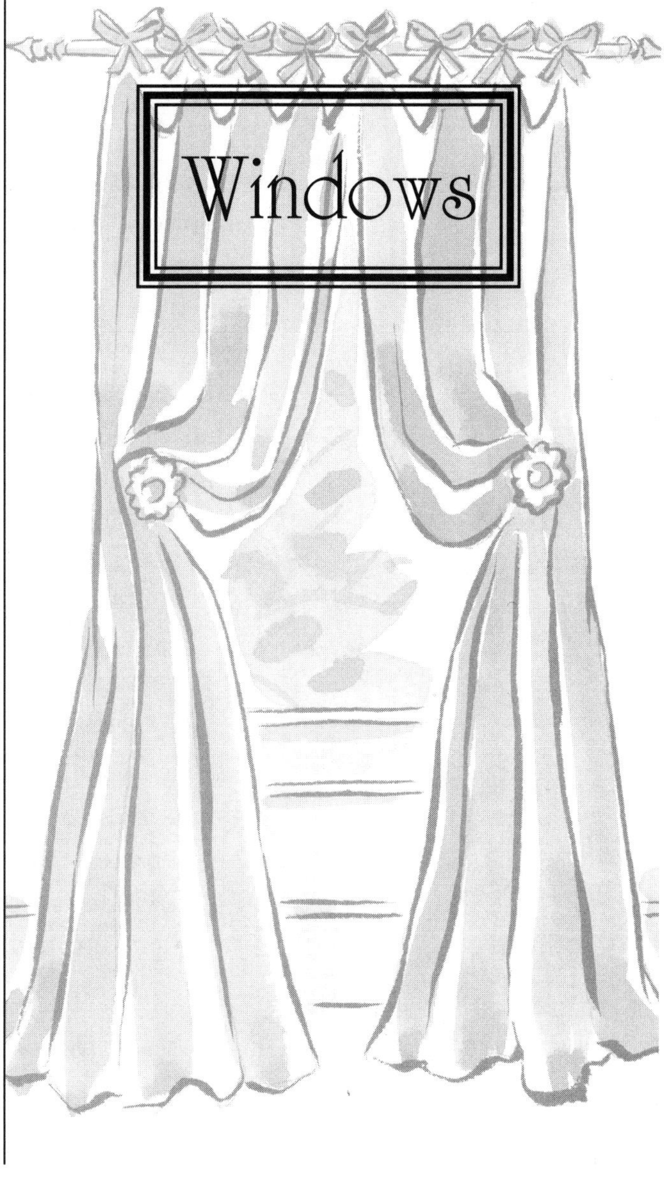

Most people think purely about looks when they address a naked window. What will be prettier—curtains, shades, or blinds? Valance or no valance? What color? What fabric? What print?

In truth, the first question should usually be: What do I want this particular window treatment to accomplish?

Your answer, which may vary from room to room, could include any of the following:

- Partial privacy
- Total privacy
- Filtering sunlight
- Blocking sunlight
- Admitting as much light as possible
- Framing a good view

- Blocking out an unattractive view
- Turning the window into a focal point
- Making the window look taller or larger
- Making a low ceiling appear higher

Once you've decided on the window treatment's jobs, your range of options becomes manageable.

Assume, for example, that you want your dining room to get natural light, but you also want partial privacy from the house next door. Sheer curtains are a natural solution; they admit sunlight while veiling the neighbors' view of your dinner hour. Sheers are usually quite simple and inexpensive to make.

You could also consider a café curtain that covers the bottom half of the window; or a classic schoolhouse-style blind that pulls up from the bottom. Both offer a measure of privacy while allowing light to spill in over the top.

Three suggestions:

- If you fall in love with a patterned fabric, unroll a couple of yards in the store and pleat it with your fingers. How does the pattern look when the fabric is gathered, as it will be at your windows? Some prints look graceful on the bolt, but dense and confusing when they fall in folds. This simple test will let you know now, before you buy.

- Try to have an expert custom-make any but the most straightforward curtains, even if you have to economize on fabric to do so. Good construction really shows.

• When in doubt about a curtain style, choose simplicity. It often costs less and is easier to achieve without mistakes.

THE HIGH-TENSION SOLUTION

For the simplest curtain imaginable, install a tension rod in the window. Sold at hardware stores, it's kept in place by springs; no hardware is needed. Some tension rods are thick, which is best for anything other than a light flutter of a curtain; others are delicately thin, which will support a light café curtain or sheer but not much else.

GLAMOUR-DISGUISE FOR TENSION RODS

To conceal the fact that you're using a tension rod, make a fabric tube two and a half times as long as the rod and just wide enough to slide the rod inside. The fabric, richly gathered from end to end along the rod, will look gorgeous. Now use brass or wooden rings to attach the curtain. It won't slide freely, but you can keep it pulled back with a tieback.

A ROD WITH HEFT

Plain wooden rods need some visual weight or they risk looking like broomsticks. Try a 3-inch-diameter pole; if it's too massive for your window treatments, downsize to 2 1/4 inches—but nothing thinner.

A TOUCH OF THE ORIENT

Use a length of bamboo to hold up lightweight curtains, especially sheers. Bamboo is typically sold at wholesale flower markets—which will often make surreptitious sales to consumers. (If you have no luck, ask a good florist to order the bamboo from his supplier.) In New York's flower market, centered around Sixth Avenue and 28th Street, I found 7-foot-long bamboo poles, some almost as thick as my wrist, selling for $5 apiece—a very low investment for a most exotic look.

DRESS UP THE RODS

Some people spend a fortune on fabric, then ignore the pole. Don't! Spray it black, white, or gold, or paint it with stripes.

For a striped rod, start with a base coat of white paint. (Begin with primer, if you're using an unfinished wood pole.) When dry, wrap it with blue masking tape in the desired width—try 1½ inches, if in doubt. Wrap the tape either in straight circles around the rod or in a continuous spiral, like a barber pole. Sand the exposed parts lightly.

Now, paint a second color—black is a classic—between the strips of tape. Remove the tape while the paint is still tacky.

Tip: *Rings will slide more easily on a shiny surface, so use semigloss or high-gloss paint.*

ALTERNATIVE RODS

For a change from wood, designers have hung curtains from copper tubing, sold at plumbing supply shops, and from birch branches, peeled or unpeeled. Even the simple black iron rods available from mail-order catalogs (see "The Best Mail-Order Resources," Appendix B) can make a curtain look particularly crisp.

THE DRIVEN SNOW

A white sheet makes a curtain so simple and pristine, no one has to realize it was meant for bedding. Use the top hem as a rod pocket, or sew standard wooden curtain rings, sold at fabric stores, to the top of the sheet. Make a new bottom hem between 4 and 12 inches deep, allowing for 2 extra inches of length so that the curtain kisses the floor.

To avoid looking skimpy, a curtain should be two and a half or even three times as wide as the window. To help with your calculations, here are standard sheet sizes:

Full-size flat sheet:	81 inches wide, 96 inches long
Queen-size flat sheet:	90 inches wide, 102 inches long
King-size flat sheet:	108 inches wide, 102 inches long

Tip: *Iron but do not launder the sheets before you sew; washing will make the fabric permanently limp. Dry clean the curtains if necessary.*

Recipe for a puddle

THE WHITEST CURTAIN

To make a pure white sheet look exquisitely pristine at the window, employ contrast: Give it a wide black border at the bottom, and hang it from a pole and rings that you have painted black.

RECIPE FOR A PUDDLE

Curtains that spill onto a floor are notoriously hard to keep clean, but if you love the look, add 6 to 8 extra inches to the curtains' length. More practical is the curtain that dusts the floor; for this, add just 1 to 2 extra inches. Beware the curtain that doesn't quite reach the floor; it can look as gangly as trousers that just skim the ankle.

ANTIQUE LINENS

For the ultimate delicacy in white curtains, suggests La Jolla, California, designer Carol Olten, use vintage or antique sheets (or long table linens) with white-on-white embroidery or a monogram. To echo the effect in the rest of your decorating, have throw pillows made from vintage white napkins. Remember to inspect closely for yellowing or stains when buying old linens.

Tip: *How do you make a curtain-rod pocket and still preserve the decorative edge of a scalloped or embroidered piece of antique linen? Sew a strip of muslin to the back and slip the rod behind it.*

THE VERSATILE SHEET

To coordinate your curtains and bed linens without that decorated-with-sheets look, borrow a technique from the editors of *House Beautiful:* Use a white sheet for the curtain, then border its bottom hem with a fat band of pattern that you cut from a top sheet or from the edges of pillowcases. (You can make tiebacks from the same pattern, if you like.) The border adds weight to the curtain, creating extra body, and it will also relate to the sheets on your bed without being too obvious about it.

***Tip:** You can sometimes shape the top edge of this patterned border by snipping around the printed design on the sheet. For example, a* House Beautiful *editor carefully cut around the black and white roses of a Ralph Lauren print—instead of slicing through them for an even band of fabric—so the flowers appeared to bloom, trompe l'oeil–style, against the white curtain.*

RECIPE FOR A CAFÉ CURTAIN

Covering only the lower third or half of a window, the café curtain originated in restaurants so that diners could be free from scrutiny yet not sacrifice their entire view. It works just as well at home. The simplest version: a narrow brass or white rod combined with standard brass clip-on rings (both are available at any hardware or fabric store). The rings open when you squeeze them, then clamp shut on the fabric. As for the curtain itself, make a rectangle of fabric two and a half times as wide as the window to create dense gathering. Alternatively, use less material—but a more translucent fabric—for a lighter, fluttery effect. Have weights sewn into the hem to give the curtain better body.

THE PINNED-UP CURTAIN

Instead of using a traditional fabric tieback, try *pinning* your curtains back.

Make a flat, ungathered curtain, sized to hang in the window like

The pinned-up curtain

a straight banner. It should have a different fabric on each side (like two handkerchiefs sewn together), though no proper lining or interlining are needed. Hang from a tension rod.

To pin the material back, grasp the lower left corner of the banner and pull it up toward the top right corner. (Or go from lower right to the upper left, if it looks better.) When you're pleased with the effect, pin the fabric in place. (Try that huge brooch of your grandmother's.) This creates a delicate drape and shows off the contrasting fabrics as well.

THE HALF-VEILED WINDOW

Another way to admit light through the top half of a window while obscuring the bottom is to hang a single fabric panel that's translucent on top, opaque below. The top half might be a loosely woven linen, muslin, or gauze; the bottom half could be a more tightly woven linen or cotton. Let it hang straight like a window shade, rather than gathered. For the most clean-lined and contemporary effect, use two fabrics of an identical light color, preferably white.

THE MINIMALIST DRAPE

Marcia Sherrill, a New York accessories and interior designer, came up with this budget trick: To dress a large window inexpensively, buy a painter's off-white canvas drop cloth and a strong wooden rod. Cut the drop cloth in half (creating two curtain panels), and stitch new, neater hems all the way around both panels—or have a tailor do it, as Sherrill did. Sew canvas ribbons, made from the cuttings, to the top hems. Tie the drop-cloth panels to the rod with bows, and let the panels puddle on the floor. The curtain, simultaneously stiff and rumpled, will have extraordinary body.

THE PERFECTLY UNBALANCED WINDOW

Curtain panels, like earrings, traditionally match—but all rules are made to be broken once in a while. The editors of *Metropolitan Home*

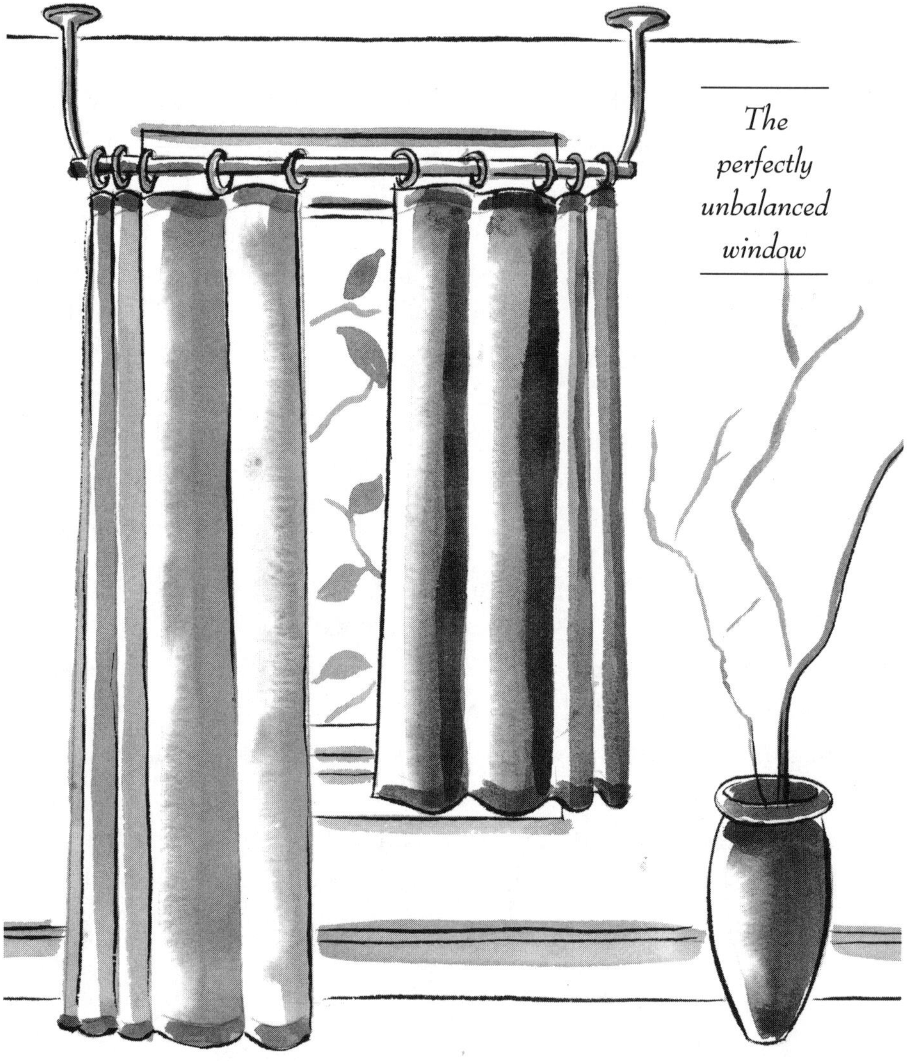

The perfectly unbalanced window

once dressed all the windows in one room with blue panels on the right, wheat-colored panels on the left. For a pair of windows on the same wall, you could also make the two outer panels (at the far left and far right) one color, and the inner panels another.

Here's an even nervier variation, inspired by New York drapery designer Mary Bright: Cut one panel at each window to the length of the sill, and let the second panel dust the floor. (Experiment with pins and proportions to see what looks best in your room.)

Tip: *Mismatched curtain panels look best when the windows themselves are symmetrically placed in the wall.*

BELT THE CURTAINS BACK

To tie back her own black and white curtains, Marcia Sherrill dug into her closet and came up with gold chain belts. Wrapped around the curtains and looped around standard tiebacks attached to the wall, the belts bring a touch of high fashion to the windows.

INSTANT DRAPERY

For truly no-sew, no-hardware curtains, try this set designer's trick, from Boston design consultants C&J Katz: Nail two lengths of fabric, one for each curtain panel, along the very top, front surface of the window frame. To get a deep luscious drape, allow 3 inches of fabric for every inch between the nails; that is, if your nails are 6 inches apart, let 18 inches of fabric drape between them. Tie ribbon bows around the nailheads for camouflage, and deeply puddle the curtains on the floor, tucking unsewn hems underneath.

ADD DIMENSION TO CURTAIN FABRIC

To make inexpensive curtain fabric look more substantial, quilt it by outlining its print on a sewing machine, suggests Linda L. Floyd, a San Francisco interior designer. Use thread to match the fabric background. The curtain will look heavier, almost as if it were lined.

Tip: *Choose an overscaled and well-defined print to make the quilting easier.*

BLOWING IN THE WIND

Most people make sheers from extremely wide (118-inch) curtain fabric, to avoid conspicuous seams. But Carey Reid Kirk, a designer

Instant drapery

in Arlington, Virginia, likes to hang individual banners of sheer fabric instead, one next to the other, so they flutter like veils in the breeze.

This looks most poetic when the fabric falls straight or is only slightly gathered. Kirk, who recently draped a long wall of side-by-side windows, used lengths of 54-inch-wide sheer fabric. (You can find narrower widths in your fabric store's dressmaker section.) When the wind picks up, each veil stirs and flutters on its own—a more evocative and fragile look than one vast curtain lifting, like a sail, into the center of the room.

Tip: *Sheer polyester, often called by its French name,* tergal, *is less luxuriant than silk but easier to clean.*

THE ALTERNATIVE CURTAIN

Curtain designers are often intrigued by unusual fabrics that drape handsomely. Men's shirting, for example, sold at fabric stores, makes a crisp-looking and lightweight curtain.

So does rayon: "It has a sheen similar to silk," says Catherine Revland, a New York drapery designer and author of *Window Chic,* an excellent source for curtain ideas and inspiration.

So does lightweight wool fabric designed for suits. And while you're shopping, look at the *reverse* side of any fabric that pleases you. Many top designers will occasionally use fabric wrong-side up—either for the actual curtains and upholstery, or just as a coordinating trim—because they like the reverse side.

DRESSING THE DORMER WINDOW

Windows in dormers sometimes look awkward or small, so the simpler the treatment, the better. Try a long sheer curtain hanging from a brass curtain rod. The sheer material might be a panel of lace or a semitranslucent linen. Delicacy can be a virtue here; you might, for example, want to sew ribbons or ties to the top of the curtain panel and tie it to the rod. Well-made wooden shutters work nicely in dormers; so do fabric blinds.

Strong colors and patterns can make a diminutive window look even smaller. Your best bets are tone-on-tone prints, such as a beige-on-beige stripe; or pale solid-color fabric.

THE SCREENING CURTAIN

The new dark fiberglass mesh that's now used for window screens has a graceful drape to it, just like good translucent fabric. And that's how Mollie Seaman, a designer with Home Depot in Quincy, Massachusetts, uses it: draped in long sophisticated swags over the tops of windows. To help it swoop, she advises, install a small piece of curtain hardware, aptly called a butterfly, at each top corner of the window frame. Wrap the material around the butterflies, and the swag will fall gracefully between them.

The mesh can also hang, densely gathered, as a modern and architectural sheer curtain.

Fiberglass screening comes in silver-gray and charcoal, in varying widths and lengths—all of them inexpensive. (At Home Depot, 100 feet of yard-wide screening costs less than $40.)

ADDING HEIGHT WITH CURTAINS

To make a room appear taller, hang the curtain rods high. Measure the distance between the top of the window frame and the ceiling, and place the rod at the halfway point—or higher, if it looks good. Let the curtains dust the floor.

THE DRAPERY SWITCH

For a window that receives no direct sunlight, you can have a reversible curtain made—one pattern for spring and summer, perhaps, and one for the darker months. (It won't work in a sunny window, because sunshine makes fabric fade.) Switching from flowers to stripes, or from white to green, will dramatically change the mood of a room.

GIVE A CURTAIN GOOD BONES

If you are investing in good custom curtains and need to economize, cut back on the fabric, not the structure, advises drapery designer Mary Bright. Instead of $100-a-yard silk, she suggests, try wool or inexpensive linen. Don't skimp on the lining, which protects the curtain fabric from sun, or the interlining, which adds weight and substance.

TOO MANY FINIALS

If you are hanging curtains across three or four side-by-side windows, the wall can get cluttered with finials. New York designer Marshall Watson suggests doing away with them altogether. He buys specialized rods (from any home decorating store) that curve in at each end and attach directly to the wall. Professionals call this "returning the rod to the wall," and it produces a neat, tailored look.

ALL THAT GLITTERS

To make a curtain dressier (and more unusual), collect chandelier crystals from flea markets, where they are often heaped into boxes and sold individually for a song. Stitch them a few inches apart

All that glitters

along the bottom of a valance or swag, so they dangle in the sunlight. Or sew them along the inside edges of your curtain panels, so they hang like a fringe. They will catch the light and make the room sparkle.

FROM THE BOTTOM UP

Basic white schoolhouse window shades will have a startling elegance if they pull up from the bottom. Any store that supplies shades and shutters can provide them. In addition to good looks, pull-up shades have a functional advantage: If pulled up only halfway, they let in light and sky views at the top of the window, while providing privacy at the lower level where you need it most.

JEWELRY FOR CURTAINS

Curtain rods traditionally end in decorative finials, which can be anything from simple wooden spheres to gilded arrowheads. These have terrific decorative value. For example, a metal rod in a sophisticated Chicago high-rise could culminate in a spiky twist of metal—while in a Nantucket beach house, it might end in a carved seashell. If anything, the finials are more important than the rod, being both visible and expressive. They need not be expensive; you can easily find unusual ones through mail-order catalogs (see "The Best Mail-Order Resources," Appendix B) or home decorating stores.

Jewelry for curtains

SHADES OF MEANING

Any fabric you love can be laminated by a shade supplier to an ordinary vinyl window shade. Your choice could be as playful as a pattern of teacups, as subtle as a taupe-on-taupe stripe.

Tip: *If you like your rooms to coordinate, use the same fabric pattern, in the same or a different color, elsewhere in the room—a table skirt, perhaps, or an oversize throw pillow. You can also repeat it as an accent in an adjoining room.*

FABRIC SHUTTERS

At the Kips Bay show house one year, New York designer Mariette Himes Gomez created a fabric shutter of such simplicity and serenity that it's still being talked about—and copied.

Each pair of shutters consists of two white, slightly translucent fabric panels, held taut by rods at the top and bottom. Because the rods are hinged, you can swing the panels to either side of the window, exposing the view. When closed, the fabric still admits some light.

Gomez had her hinged rods custom made, but you don't have to. Call any supplier listed in the Yellow Pages under "Drapery and Curtain Fixtures," and ask if they carry swing-out rods. A common type adjusts in length between 15 and 22 inches. You can order similar fixtures, called crane rods, from the Country Curtains catalog (see

"The Best Mail-Order Resources," Appendix B), though only three lengths are available—12, 18, and 24 inches. Be sure they precisely fit your windows before ordering.

THE RADIATOR OBSTACLE

Long curtains can fall awkwardly from a window that has a radiator directly underneath. Instead, many designers use fabric blinds that offer some of the softness of curtains. Among the options:

- Fabric laminated to an ordinary window shade, from any shade supplier
- Tailored Roman blinds, which fall in neat horizontal pleats
- Ornate Austrian blinds, with a rich swagged look
- A fabric-covered valance set above wooden blinds

ARCHITECTURAL WINDOWS

One of the priciest window investments, but also one of the best looking, is shutters—custom-made plantation shutters with slats that can be raised or lowered. Sunlight pouring through the slats will cast dramatic shadows on the ceiling or floor, and shutters can make any window seem more important. To disguise one client's meager windows, New York designer Stan Hura ran plantation shutters across the entire wall, from ceiling to floor. The shutters remain closed, implying a mass of windows, while the louvers tilt open, admitting daylight.

__Tip:__ Don't try to economize on shutters.
Inexpensive ones look cheap,
and the unfinished variety can be a nightmare to paint.

HOLLYWOOD WINDOWS

In film noir set design, windows were often dressed in wooden blinds. These need to be custom made, as they should fit neatly inside the window frame. The most substantial-looking version has 2-inch-deep slats; check to see if your window is deep enough to hold them. Order blinds in a color that most closely matches your floorboards—or if you have wall-to-wall carpeting, order any color that pleases you, including black or white.

As for the fabric tapes that run down the front, they come in dozens of colors and such patterns as tapestry and paisley. Consider white for airiness, or black for its 1940s glamour. I've used white tapes to emphasize the spaciousness in a large yellow room, and black tapes to emphasize the coziness of a small red room. Both look terrific.

THE TOO-BRIGHT ROOM

If your windows face south, the heat and glare can be overwhelming. (It can also fade your furniture and paintings and force you to crank up the air conditioning, raising your energy bills.) You can reduce the sunlight, without cutting off the view, by using window shades made of Mylar—a dark see-through plastic film—behind your regular curtains or blinds. In terms of room-darkening power, it's equivalent to putting on sunglasses. In winter just roll it up. Shade suppliers can make these to order.

A PAINTED WINDOW FRAME

Van-Martin Rowe, a Pasadena designer, likes to frame windows with a handpainted border. Make it 6 to 9 inches wide, he suggests, neatly encircling the entire window molding. If there's room on top, paint a triangular pediment. Use a solid color or any handpainted design that pleases you. For a rustic look, paint the border freehand, over a penciled outline; its tiny imperfections will add to the charm.

PRIVACY THROUGH GLASS

Curtains aren't the only route to privacy. To veil a window without losing light, Van-Martin Rowe adds a layer of obscure glass. This type of glass is translucent but not transparent; glass suppliers offer it ribbed, leaded, industrial (with chicken wire inside), or even

Privacy through glass

beveled. Rowe orders little rectangles, sized to fit over each small pane in his window, in a mix of styles. He then affixes each piece of obscure glass directly to the window glass, holding it in place with silicone (sold at hardware stores) around the edges.

Often he fills in only the lower half of the window for privacy, and leaves the top half transparent.

Tip: *If the mullions of your window are painted white, use white silicone; if they are any other color, use clear silicone.*

CHAPTER 4

Problem Rooms, Great Solutions

A problem room is any room whose features bother you or make furniture arrangements difficult. The ceiling may be too low, windows too few, or walls overpunctuated by doorways. You could renovate—but it's more practical, and more affordable, to make the problem visually recede through good interior decorating.

A designer's job, in fact, consists largely of solving problems. If it's done well, you can't spot the room's original flaw, or even pick out the solution. Handsome low-slung cabinetry, for example, may look purely aesthetic, when in fact it exists to conceal an ignoble radiator and handle an overflow of storage. Ceiling-high curtains may look glorious; in fact, they could be the designer's way of implying taller windows. And a weathered terracotta finish may make walls look aged and Italian—but it can also be employed to disguise new Sheetrock or camouflage pitted plaster.

One way to train your eye to spot and fix problems is to scrutinize the "before" pictures when you visit a decorator show house; they often reveal design dilemmas you can't see in the finished room. At the illustrious Kips Bay Boys and Girls Club Decorator Show House in New York, for example, the designer Clodagh affixed big pots of golden bamboo outside the window of a tiny sitting room. Visitors, engaged by the exotic effect, barely noticed the air shaft beyond—or realized that a problematic view was being beautifully resolved before their eyes.

A few thoughts on solutions for difficult rooms:

- Don't be afraid to paint small rooms in dark or intense colors. It plays on their best feature—intimacy—and, surprisingly, often opens them up.
- Put at least one piece of overscaled furniture in a small room. That, too, can make the space seem larger.
- If you can't disguise a flaw, draw attention to something else. Create a focal point with furnishings to distract from the lack of windows; invest in a gorgeous vintage rug to distract from walls in poor condition. (This is particularly valid for renters.)

HEIGHTEN A ROOM WITH PICTURES

To combat a low ceiling, stack pictures three or even four high, so that the top picture in the stack nearly touches the ceiling (or the molding at the top of the wall). Alternatively, create a rising pyramid of pictures above the sofa. The impact of these tall arrangements will fool your eye into perceiving a tall room.

HEIGHTEN A ROOM WITH PAINT

Carry a pale ceiling color 12 inches down onto walls that are slightly darker in tone. This turns the ceiling into a lid that's visually lifted by the subtle color contrast. Try a white ceiling over biscuit-colored walls, for example, or a very pale sky-blue ceiling over taupe.

THE CONTEMPORARY FIREPLACE

That huge open space over the fireplace can be daunting to fill, especially when you consider the cost of a massive, gilt-framed mirror. Here's a modern solution that costs less: Have a mirror supplier install a single slice of mirror that fills the entire space, edge to edge and all the way up to the ceiling. (Have the installer do the measuring, in case the chimney breast isn't perfectly symmetrical.) The room will seem brighter and more airy, and the mirror will look sufficiently tailored to share the space with antiques.

THE WALLPAPER LIFT

You can visually bump up a low ceiling by affixing a wallpaper border to the edge of the ceiling where it meets the wall (rather than at the top of the wall). To keep the effect subtle, choose a wallpaper border in largely soft or neutral colors that won't contrast sharply with the walls.

BRING IN THE SKY ON A BUDGET

For a less expensive "window" overhead, paint the ceiling soft beige or any pale color; then, in the middle, paint a large pure-white rectangle. That simple white shape—an idea that New York designer Glenn Gissler used to dramatically enlarge an attic show-house room—evokes a skylit ceiling.

Tip: *How large a rectangle you paint depends on the size and proportions of your room. Imagine that you're installing an oversize skylight, or the partially glass roof of an artist's garret. If you still don't trust your eye, make a rectangle out of paper (not newsprint; the ink rubs off), and tape it to the ceiling as a test.*

BRING IN THE SKY

Here's another way to visually raise a low ceiling: Hire a decorative artist to paint a perfect circle of sky and clouds overhead, perfectly centered. The circle can be bordered with trompe l'oeil molding, though you and the artist will want to work out the details and proportions. The effect will be as startling and as liberating as if you had sliced through the roof. Consider this an investment, as you are commissioning a personal piece of artwork.

SPACE-EXPANDING COLOR

Some rooms are so small that nothing really makes them seem larger. Indeed, such rooms can foster intimacy and great conversation—why fight the size that creates the atmosphere? Instead, paint an impossibly small room in the passionate color of your choice. (Terry Trucco, a *New York Times* design columnist, did this in her bedroom with midnight-blue walls.) The room will seem to embrace you like a cloak—and believe it or not, it may feel larger, as the color will completely distract you from the size.

MIRROR THE SPACE

When Washington, D.C., designer Barry Dixon encounters a small room, he sometimes leans a tall mirror against the wall. It expands the room, he explains, by reflecting a good deal of the ceiling. The mirror should be at least 6 feet tall and framed in something classic (gold, silver, or black). For an added touch of elegance, have the glass beveled. Such a mirror will not be inexpensive, but it will make a stunning contribution to any room that surrounds it.

EXPOSE THE FLOOR

A small room will seem larger if your furniture reveals as much of the floor as possible.

Glass tables are an ideal choice; they can look modern or antique,

Mirror the space

Expose the floor

depending on the type of metal base you choose. "Leggy" furniture is also ideal—if you are slipcovering an armchair, for example, choose a short skirt that leaves the legs exposed. In a small bedroom, avoid chunky nightstands; try a slender pedestal table or mount a shelf instead.

BIG IMAGE, SMALL ROOM

A round convex mirror—the kind that bulges outward—reflects a greatly expanded view of the surrounding room. This is intriguing anywhere, but can also help a small room make a big first impression. Hang the mirror on the wall facing the doorway, so that one of the first things you see upon entering the room is the bull's-eye reflection.

Tip: *Many convex mirrors have carved antique frames, but new ones of less-expensive cast resin can often be found in stores (or catalogs), such as The Bombay Company. Buy the largest you can afford.*

THE LUXURY OF A DOUBLE DOOR

One small stroke of renovation—the widening of a doorway—can bring a tremendous sense of spaciousness to a small house or apartment. Choose one prominent doorway, and have it cut to double its size. You can arch it if you like, or fill the opening with two French

The luxury of a double door

doors. Either way, this architectural gesture will make the surrounding rooms feel more generous, and enhance the sense of flow from room to room.

THE ENDLESS HALLWAY

Mark Hampton, whose clients include George and Barbara Bush, will sometimes break up a long hallway's tunnellike quality by installing pilasters along its length. (Pilasters are flat columns, sometimes fluted, that extend about an inch from the wall.)

A budget alternative? Stencil pilasters right on the wall. You can find dramatic architectural stencils in mail-order catalogs like The Stencil Collector (see "The Best Mail-Order Reources," Appendix B). Other tall stencils may work just as well: palm trees, with their lanky trunks, or pedestals topped with statuesque urns.

Have the pilasters or tree trunks face each other down the hall. To set the scale, arrange the key ones so they flank the doorways. If extras are needed in between, insert them symmetrically.

The endless hallway

Tip: *Pilasters look best in pairs. You'll probably get a better result at home if you don't experiment with odd numbers.*

THE ENDLESS HALLWAY II

Have a carpenter build bookshelves the length of the hall or in a long stretch between two doorways. Mark Hampton uses a turn-of-the-century proportion that looks gracious but takes up little space: He makes the bookshelves just 9 inches deep, so they don't steal much floor space, and runs them just 5 feet high. Stand photographs and vases on top of the shelves, and hang pictures on the wall above.

THE ENDLESS HALLWAY III

Sometimes the best thing to do with a long tedious hallway is divide it into two shorter ones. You can do this beautifully with a portiere—a floor-length curtain, traditionally used in doorways. Between a fabric store and a hardware store, you'll find all the materials you need.

A portiere needs to look pretty from both sides, though the sides don't have to match. (You might have a floral fabric back-to-back with a solid.) Unlike a formal window drapery, a simple portiere is easily made. You may need only one curtain panel, if the hallway is narrow and the fabric wide. Sew large wooden rings along the top.

Before you hang the portiere, however, dress up the rod. Slip it

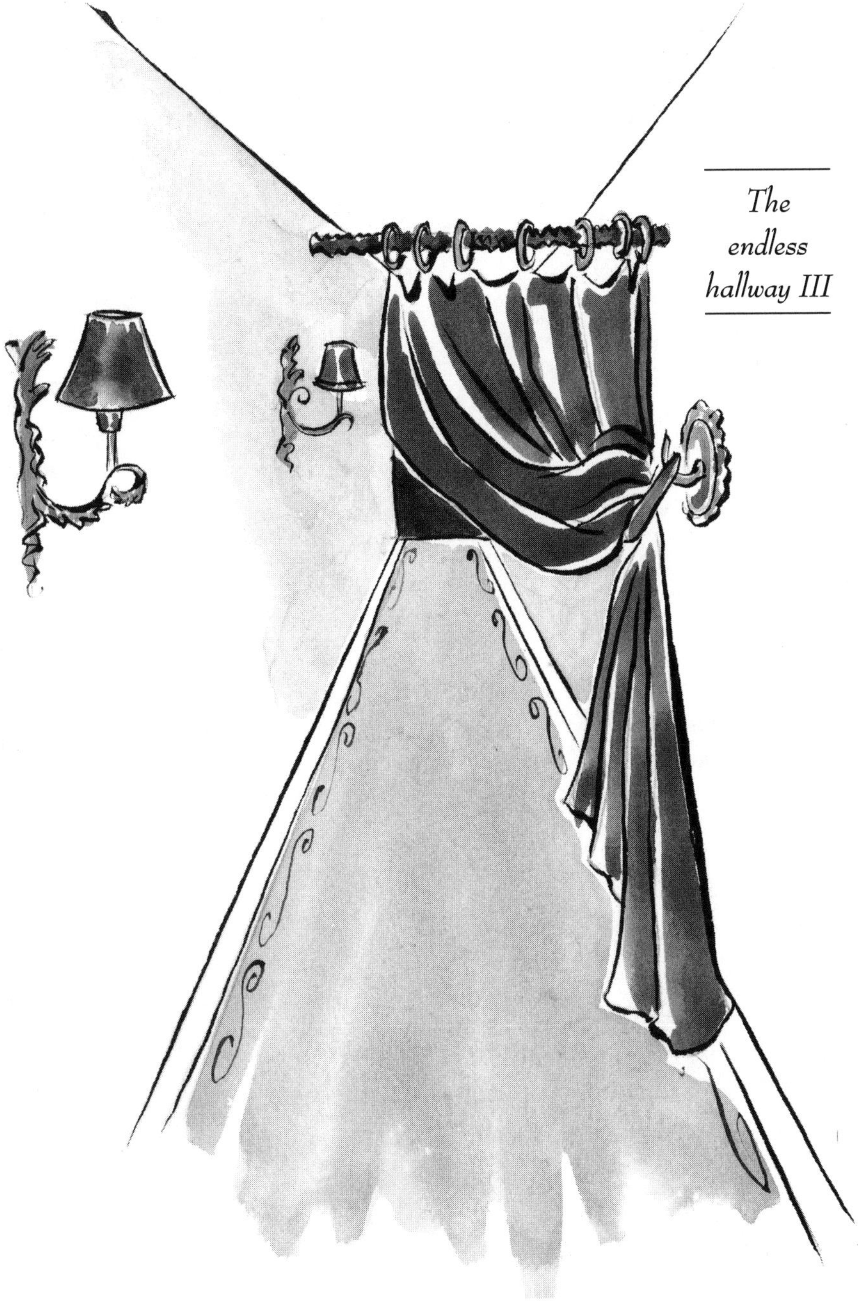

The endless hallway III

into a sleeve—a fabric tube that's two and a half times longer than the rod. Over this sleeve, which will be tightly gathered, you can now slide (well, coax) the curtain rings with the portiere attached.

BEEF UP THE MOLDINGS

If your moldings seem skinny, don't rush to replace them (a sizable expense). Instead, paint a narrow band of color in the crevice or on the curve of the molding. Make the band about half an inch or 1 inch wide, in a color of your choice—dark taupe is a good conservative choice, but you can go brighter, perhaps keying the color to the rug or a powerful painting. The stripe of color will give the molding new prominence.

Tip: *Use blue masking tape, which will keep your lines straight without lifting paint off the walls when you pull it up. Remove the tape while the paint is still damp.*

UPGRADING SHEETROCK

Even in a million-dollar house, wallboard walls look—well, like wallboard. Most designers upgrade it by hiring a plasterer to layer on a few thin coats of plaster, a process called skim-coating. It's expensive, but that veneer gives the walls a look of real solidity.

UPGRADING SHEETROCK II

Milk paint, which dates back to King Tutankhamen's tomb and was popular on early American furniture, can put an intriguing coarse finish over wallboard. (Apply a coat of latex primer first.) Made of milk protein, pigments, and other natural ingredients, milk paint is sold in barn red, pumpkin, mustard, and other historic shades, both strong and muted. It comes in powder form; mix with water, and you've got paint.

To order, or for the name of a distributor, *contact:* Old-Fashioned Milk Paint Company, 436 Main Street, Groton, MA, 01450; (508) 448-6336.

WHEN THE ROOM NEEDS MORE WINDOWS

To keep a room with no view or with a paucity of windows from feeling claustrophobic, create a focal point that serves instead of a view. In a living room whose windows were few and annoyingly small, writer and decorator Tracie Rozhon installed an antique mantelpiece and hung an oversize gilt-framed mirror above. Because the visitor's eyes are drawn straight to this imposing hearth, the lack of windows is barely apparent.

Tip: *When you dress the windows, keep the treatments simple so as not to compete with the room's new focal point.*

When a room needs more windows

INSTANT ARCHITECTURE

The most important trim in a room is the baseboard and crown molding. But don't forget the chair rail, a stock molding found in any lumberyard. Encircle the room with it (install it 36 inches above the floor), and use two closely related shades of paint on the wall—one above the chair rail, one below.

INSTANT ARCHITECTURE II

To get the effect of wedding-cake moldings without paying for them, install two lengths of molding under the ceiling, 3 or 4 inches apart. (The top one, a few inches below the ceiling, should be slightly fancier than the bottom one.) The band of wall space between them will now read as one facet of a statuesque molding. Paint it white, like the trim itself.

BRIGHTEN A DARK FOYER

Add drama and height to a tiny entry hall by mirroring the ceiling, suggests designer Barbara Southerland of Greenville, North Carolina, and New York City. If the foyer is particularly tiny, the mirror installer may be able to use a single sheet of mirror, with an opening cut for the ceiling fixture. Otherwise, have the ceiling mirrored in four quadrants that meet at the lighting fixture.

Tip: *Make sure that your overhead light does not aim bare bulbs at the ceiling, or the mirror will reflect mostly glare.*

HELP A SUN-STARVED ROOM

If a room receives little sunlight, you may be tempted to paint it white. But white can look lackluster and even scruffy in a dim room. Instead, try a light pastel in a warm tone, such as yellow, pink, or peach. Even the subtle presence of color will brighten the room.

THE GRAPHIC STAIR

To turn an awkwardly placed or too-narrow stairway into a modern architectural asset, paint the risers (the vertical sections), or the entire staircase, in a startling but beautiful color. It will give the stairs the quality of geometric sculpture.

Tip: *Wipe the stairs down with paint thinner to remove any traces of wax. Buy oil-based floor paint, which dries exceptionally hard, and thin the first coat 10 to 15 percent with paint thinner. The second and third coats can be diluted slightly less, but the diluting is critical—thick oil paint won't dry properly.*

MAKING USE OF AWKWARD DORMERS

What advantage can you squeeze from a tight, recessed space that gracefully holds a window but not much else? Built-ins are a great solution here, allowing you to take advantage of a dormer's narrow confines and natural light. Among the possibilities:

- A little writing desk. A pair of shelves can be added above the window for books, turning the dormer into a sliver of a home office. Finishing details, like a bullnose edging along the front of the desk surface, will add class at little cost.
- Bookshelves that reach the windowsill, so that the top of the shelving unit acts as an extended sill for display.
- A window seat, with storage below the seat and a custom-made cushion above.
- A dressing table—much like the desk, but consider curving the front so it arcs toward the room. It will have a more sensual appearance than the workmanlike angles of a desk. Natural light from the window will be a real bonus here.

Tip: *For a dressing table,*
add a half-inch-thick glass top.

Making use of awkward dormers

THE DINING AREA DILEMMA

An L-shaped living room, with the el designed for dining, may feel too contemporary or too open if you have traditional tastes. One way to imply a separation of rooms without building an actual wall is to curtain off the el with drapery. The drapery can be formal, with a valance and professionally constructed curtains, or it can be a do-it-yourself project with translucent silk sheers that hang from a rod or track. The curtains can be tied back, or they can be parted just enough to imply a doorway in the middle.

DINING AREA DILEMMA II

To suggest a separate dining room in an L-shaped space, hang an important-looking arrangement of prints or pictures in the el—and end it abruptly just where the dining area ends. In her own home Los Angeles designer Kate Stamps hung three symmetrical rows of nineteenth-century portraits in her dining area; the wall continues into her living room, but where the portraits stop, a boundary is subtly enforced.

DINING AREA DILEMMA III

Use a pair of tall handsome bookcases to frame the opening to a dining el—another Kate Stamps solution. Built-ins work best here, serving as partial walls that narrow the broad opening into some-

Dining area dilemma II

thing of a doorway; the implication is that a separate little room lies beyond. Freestanding shelves can also work, though not as well, because baseboard moldings create a visibly awkward space between shelving units and walls.

DINING AREA DILEMMA IV

If the main living area is white, paint the dining el—including its ceiling—an entirely different color. (Leave the moldings white.) Because the el is probably small, this is a good place to indulge your color fantasies.

CARVING OUT A FOYER

In some modern apartments the front door opens directly, if not very graciously, into the living room. You can *hint* at a foyer, however, by placing a dining or library table near the front door and staging it as a hall table during the day. Keep flowers on the top, and pull dining chairs away so they're backed against the wall (a traditional thing to do with dining chairs when they're not in use). Add a small tray or ceramic dish for keys and mail, and you've implied an entry hall where none exists.

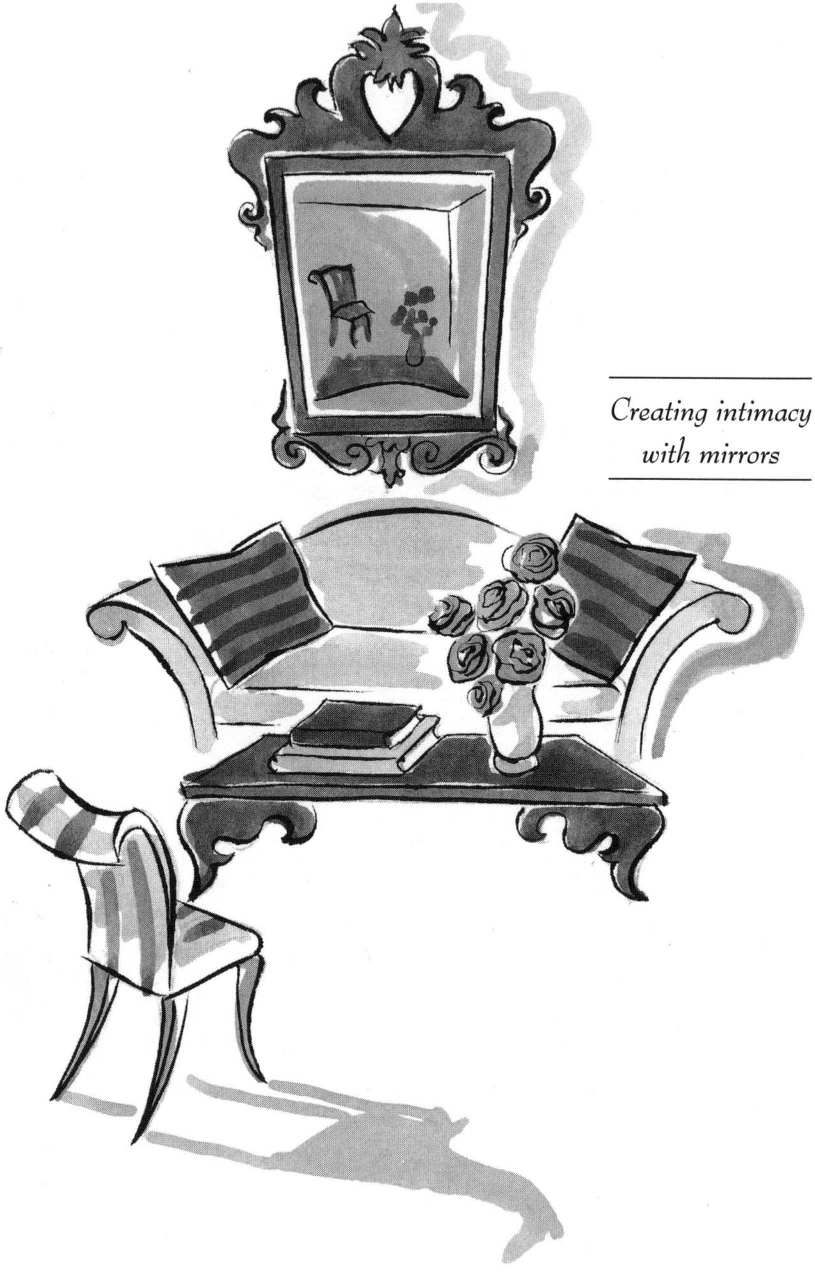

Creating intimacy with mirrors

THE INTERRUPTED ROOM

If too many doorways crowd a room, paint everything—doors, doorframes, moldings, and walls—one color. (It does not have to be white.) The walls and doors will melt into the same backdrop, so your eye won't worry the separation between them.

CREATING INTIMACY WITH MIRRORS

Large rooms are seen as a virtue, but sometimes they feel too overscaled for quiet conversation, small gatherings, or solitary reading. To help cloister off a conversation area in such a room, Washington, D.C. designer Barry Dixon hangs an ornamental mirror on the wall so it angles down, reflecting the seats—and, in the evenings, candlelight on the coffee table.

To angle the mirror down, just move the wire on the back so it's near the midpoint, not the top, of the frame.

CHAPTER ◆ 5

Home Furnishings

If you plan your home around a few good investments, you can fill in the rest with what the designer Billy Baldwin called "humbler things of good design."

In furniture, the best investment is a fabulous sofa that's plump with goosedown (or goosedown with foam in the middle, to appease the humbler budget). Its quality will show from across the room—so that even if you stir in an inexpensive halogen torchère lamp (less than $20 from a discount office-supply catalog), all eyes will remain on the sofa. (And all guests will gravitate toward it, too.) Upholstered furniture is so important, in fact, that the equation doesn't work in reverse: A visibly inexpensive sofa will bring down the look and comfort level of a room, even if you place it near a $400 Italian lamp.

If your budget is more foam than feather, here's a fairly stylish compromise: buy a simple foam-filled sofa—solid color, classic lines—and splurge on oversize down-filled throw pillows. You'll notice the plush invitation and high quality of the pillows every time you enter the room—and they'll still be gorgeous years later, when you finally have a sofa you adore.

As for the "humbler things of good design," look for furnishings with good bones, or beautiful lines, and perhaps a little age. You can economize by buying flea market tables or wooden chairs, then painting them, refinishing them, or leaving their hard-earned patina intact. Flea markets are great sources, not only because they can save you money but because they're so well stocked with vintage and antique pieces. Every room should have at least one well-aged piece of furniture—not necessarily an investment-quality antique, but something that carries a sense of the past. It will give your home character and roots.

True luxury has little to do with money. Luxury, for example, is a deep comfortable chair placed right by the fire, with a small table nearby to hold your drink and your book. It's a chaise that's slanted toward a fabulous view, or a picture you love. It's a coffee table big enough for your books, a few collectibles, dinner among friends, and even your feet. But luxury is *not* a Louis XV commode—that's grandeur, and unless you live in a palazzo, it's not essential to good decor.

CORNER THE FURNITURE

The corner of a room can be an evocative, intimate spot from which to choreograph a furniture arrangement, especially if you aren't stuck with a wide sofa. In the living room, angle a love seat so its back is to the corner. Stand a paneled screen behind it if you like—or a ficus tree, or a table with a lamp. Place a coffee table in front and, on either side of that, a comfortable chair. Now, when you walk into the room, that angled love seat issues an open invitation, and can actually make the room look bigger.

Tip: *If you use a screen, don't ignore the dead space behind it—commandeer it for storage.*

Upholstery marriages

UPHOLSTERY MARRIAGES

The chairs, sofa, and love seat in your living room should look harmonious, but not matched. To create this kind of natural affinity between furnishings, Ann Glen, an interior designer in Stonington, Connecticut, looks for upholstered pieces with rounded rather than squared lines. Her sofa cushions, accordingly, are plump with down, not rigid with foam. "A curved line looks softer and more comfortable than a straight line," says Glen. "It also unites everything. If you have a rounded-arm love seat next to a straight-arm sofa, it won't look right."

THE LUXURY TEST

True comfort means never having to get up for the things you need. Test your living room's luxury quotient: Pour yourself a drink, and sit down in every seat. Is there a convenient spot where you can set the drink down? If not, you need an occasional table (a decorator's term for a small, often ornamental table). Can you reach a reading light? If not, you probably need sconces or lamps. Finally, sit in your own favorite reading chair. What happens when the phone rings? If it involves getting up, have an electrician install an outlet for a phone extension, or keep a portable phone nearby.

Tip: *If you can't afford to have cushions stuffed with down, substitute a mix of feathers and down, or down around a core of foam. For throw pillows, you can economize further and simply use a ready-made form filled with feathers.*

THE WELL-DRESSED SOFA

Before you replace your old sofa, consider whether a slipcover might improve it—and save you money, too. Rachel Ashwell, who launched the Shabby Chic stores and wrote the Shabby Chic design book (Regan Books), favors slipcovers that are slightly baggy, usually white, and always, always machine washable and dryable. They bring a relaxed formality to the furniture, can be changed for seasonal decorating, and are easier to clean than upholstery. Here are her slipcover tips:

- The best candidate for a slipcover is a sofa that's fully upholstered (no carved wood along the top or arms), nicely shaped, and structurally sound. If it squeaks, buy a new sofa.
- The best slipcovers have welting, with all seams overlocked, or stitched twice; and they're made by slipcover specialists. (See the Yellow Pages under "Slipcovers.") Decide whether you want the covers skintight, like upholstery, or slightly loose, in the English style; or with dressmaker details like buttons, inverted kick pleats, or flouncy skirts. Magazine pictures are an ideal way to communicate your preferences.

- Choose a washable cotton fabric—a category that ranges from white denim, Ashwell's favorite, to some velvets and gloriously rumpled damasks.
- Have new zippered covers made for throw pillows, too.

THE ECONOMICAL WAY TO A TERRIFIC SOFA

A great down-filled sofa can cost $6,000 or more. If you can't spend this kind of money, spend time instead: Search flea markets or junque shops for a vintage sofa that has graceful lines and a strong frame. (No wobbles, no squeaks.) Have its seat cushions generously stuffed with down or a mix of down and feathers, and have a slipcover made. As Carol Prisant, an editor with the British design magazine *The World of Interiors,* points out, you can always spend the savings on antique wood furnishings—which, unlike upholstered pieces, are likely to hold their value.

Tip: *If you prefer the ease of buying a new sofa, you'll find good guidance in* The Couch Book *by Fayal Greene (Hearst Books).*

ZONING THE LARGE LIVING ROOM

An oversize living room typically requires two conversation areas rather than one. If you own a daybed, chaise, or hired man's bench—anything long, upholstered, and backless—try using it to divide the room. It will serve both seating areas, while subtly reinforcing the separation between the two.

ALTERNATIVE LIVING-ROOM MARRIAGES

Don't feel locked into the sofa-and-two-armchairs combination. Try a love seat with two chairs instead—or be daring and surround your coffee table with four or five deeply comfortable armchairs, and no sofa at all. Stir in several ottomans to hold books or serve as extra seating, and anchor the seating arrangement by slipping a big, handsome rug underneath.

FURNISH FOR INTIMACY

Why do spouses always end up reading at opposite ends of the house? Create a reading retreat for two by angling a pair of armchairs toward each other and letting them share a large square ottoman.

Tip: Make sure each chair has its own light source, perhaps an unobtrusive but classic pharmacy lamp, coming from the left.

RECLAIMING THE HEARTH

Most people who are fortunate enough to have a fireplace tend to build their main seating arrangement around it—sofa, coffee table, chairs. But if you don't entertain all that often, consider a more intimate alternative: Pull two armchairs or wing chairs up to the hearth instead. Place a round table between them, piled with books. The hearth now becomes an anchor for a deeply personal spot, ideal for two. (Remember to light a fire.)

RECLAIMING A WINDOW

A small table and two chairs, placed right by the living-room window, creates a private spot for coffee-drinking and newspaper-reading in a room that is often anything but intimate. It also gives people a reason to gravitate toward the window, and the chairs can be drawn up near the sofa for parties.

WHAT EVERY SOFA NEEDS

Some alternatives to the traditional coffee table:

- Two small square tables, such as tea tables, placed side by side. This looks more formal than a standard coffee table and also allows you to use antiques. (Coffee tables are a modern invention.)

- A round, possibly antique dining table (28 to 36 inches across), cut down to the appropriate height.
- A wrought-iron garden table, with a thick beveled-glass top. This not only provides a hint of the outdoors but makes the room look bigger because of its transparency.
- A round of beveled glass placed over three or four level stacks of art books can be an offhand and witty solution.
- An antique window, perhaps with leaded glass, found at an architectural salvage yard; have a carpenter make legs for it.
- An ornamental slice of wrought-iron gate (also from a salvage yard). Have a carpenter build a frame for it, with legs, and top it with half-inch-thick beveled glass.

WHAT EVERY SOFA DOESN'T NEED

If you buy a new sofa or love seat, don't keep the accompanying throw pillows. They're too small and too neatly matched to the upholstery—a combination that can rob a room of individuality. (Besides, they're probably stuffed with foam, which feels unyielding.) Instead, have your own, more gracious pillows made. (Look for pillow tips in Chapter 7.)

***Tip:** When shopping for pillow fabric, bring the cover of an old sofa pillow with you to ensure that the patterns and colors are complementary.*

OTTOMAN EMPIRE

Instead of a coffee table, consider investing in a large flat ottoman in a square or rectangular shape. The fabric has a gentler look than a table's hard surface, and the piece is more versatile: You can always commandeer it for extra seating. To serve coffee or support a vase of flowers, just keep a lacquered tray on top.

Tip: *If storage is a consideration,*
look for an ottoman that opens up like a chest.

FOR SECRET STORAGE

Consider using an antique wooden chest as a coffee table if you're short on storage, or if your sofa unfolds into a bed. The chest can store rarely used sheets and towels for guests, while its top holds magazines and drinks.

THE MAGAZINE LOVER'S COFFEE TABLE

If piles of magazines seem to grow spontaneously around your home, look for a coffee table with a display shelf under its glass top. Neatly stacked on that shelf, the magazines can be seen through the glass but won't clutter up the surface, and they'll be accessible when you curl up to read.

BRING IN THE GARDEN

A single piece of metal garden furniture can evoke the outdoors, especially in a room starved for sunlight. This works best when the piece is clearly antique, or at least patinated with age.

Tip: *You can raise the status of a garden chair by giving it a thick, well-made cushion that's trimmed with welting or other detailing. Or enhance a metal table with a better glass top—half an inch thick with a beveled edge, available from any glass supplier.*

A COLLECTION OF CHAIRS

In her book *American Country Details* (Clarkson Potter Publishers), Mary Emmerling explains how she seeks out graceful and sculptural little chairs—like ice-cream parlor chairs, with their heart-shaped wire backs—at flea markets and garage sales. Use them to decorate empty corners, she suggests, or commandeer those with hard seats as side tables. The chairs don't have to match, as each will have its own personality; and they can always be pulled up for extra seating at dinners and parties.

CHIPPENDALE WITHOUT STARCH

There's no law that says Chippendale chairs must wear damask to dinner. If you've inherited or purchased traditional dining chairs that are all formality and not enough personality, dress them down with a slightly eccentric fabric on the seat cushion. You might choose vintage 1950s tea towels, or white canvas on which you've painted your own designs with black or gold fabric paint, or even pinstriped men's suiting fabric if it's soft enough to sit on.

A GATHERING OF SMALL SEATS

Lisa Skolnik, the Chicago city editor for *Metropolitan Home* magazine, collects African tribal stools and gathers them, like miniature guests, around her fireplace. They look sculptural when not in use, serve as small pull-up tables when needed, and can double as seating when a crowd arrives.

DINING CHAIRS AS VARIED AS THE GUESTS

Who says dining chairs have to match? It's often more interesting if they suggest a gathering in progress. Different chairs require only one attribute in common. This could be color (black upholstery, for example, on modern and antique chairs). It could be height and proportion. Or it could be material, such as honey-colored cane seating on various antique seats.

Tip: *Try stirring a bench or settee into the mix.*

Dining chairs as varied as the guests

THE PAINTED DINING CHAIR

If your dining table and chairs are fairly plain and form a matching set, à la Pottery Barn or Ikea, consider making a graphic statement with color so they won't look like catalog items. Paint the chairs differently—two yellow, two periwinkle, and two rose, perhaps. Consider adding stripes in spots to create detailing or the look of dovetailing. Or paint the chairs in gradations of a single color, working down in intensity from fuscia to peony, or cobalt to sky blue, as you move around the table.

JUDGE FURNITURE BY ITS BONES

Train your eye to scour flea markets for wood furniture that's slightly battered (and therefore inexpensive) but has great lines. These pieces are often overlooked because they lack a handsome finish—which you can often supply just by painting the piece glossy black or white.

Examples: A four-poster bed in scarred brown wood (paint it white for country sweetness, black for city sophistication), a bureau (change the knobs, paint the surface) or a set of plain brown-wood chairs with torn fabric on the seats (paint the chairs, change the fabric with a staple gun). If a piece has grace, good proportions, and sturdy construction, paint will bring out its best qualities.

START WITH THE RUG

In choosing colors for walls and fabrics, many interior designers use a client's rug (often an Oriental antique) for inspiration and as a starting point. If you are fortunate enough to have a rug you love, key the room's paint and fabric colors to one or more of the hues. The rug should offer many options, from dark red to navy, green to cream.

To make a wonderful rug stand out, create contrast: Paint your walls a pale color that plays a minor role in the rug's pattern—perhaps the palest green or delicate yellow from a largely red Oriental (or, of course, white). To make the room as rich and intense as the rug, paint the walls a deeper hue that's more prominent in the pattern.

WHAT SHOULD YOU SPEND ON A RUG?

Good antique rugs cost many thousands of dollars. But you can still have something handsome on the floor for less than $1,000 if you consider sisal, summery dhurries, vintage (rather than antique) rugs, or new rugs that are up front and honest about their newness. (Patterns such as leopard or zebra or Victorian florals are excellent examples.) Just avoid the middle road—the new machine-made rug masquerading as an Oriental antique. Your guests won't be fooled, and once you've looked at more rugs, neither will you.

FIT THE RUG TO THE ROOM

To determine the largest rug a living room or bedroom can hold, subtract 3 feet from the width and length of the room.

For a dining room, you need to figure the *smallest* rug and work up from there. Add 4 feet to the width and length of the dining table to get the minimum size. Runners should be no more than four inches narrower than your hall, and 18 to 24 inches shorter.

THE DESIGNER TABLE

A round skirted table next to the sofa is handsome, useful, and affordable. It's also easily acquired: medium-density fiberboard tables are sold inexpensively at department stores and even dime stores. They can be skirted with store-bought cloths in standard sizes. Just as important, these tables can offer a solution to numerous design dilemmas:

- Nothing fills an empty corner so graciously, especially when a handsome lamp stands on the table and pictures are grouped on the wall above it.
- It makes an excellent end table for a sofa. Top it with a round of beveled glass (one half-inch thick) or mirror (one quarter-inch thick) so guests can set their drinks down without worrying.

• It's hospitable to storage: Old files, stacks of magazines, or winter sweaters are easily hidden under the skirt.

Do remember that the table will look only as good as the fabric it's draped with.

THE GENIUS OF A CONSOLE

If you have a conspicuously bare wall in a foyer, living room, or long hallway, make it a focal point with the addition of a well-placed demi-lune (half-moon) table or a long and narrow console table. Either one can set an important stage for display.

Place the table against the wall. If desired, skirt it with a fabric that's full of body, such as velvet, canvas, or linen; the space underneath the skirt will double as copious storage. Alternatively, if you rarely entertain, your console might be a gateleg table with sides that fold down like long wings. When guests arrive, clear off the top and raise the sides—instant dining table.

Arrange a few overscaled objects on the console. Among the possibilities: a cluster of tall vases, a large picture frame (or three), a gold-framed watercolor leaning against the wall, a stack of Shaker boxes, a stack of leatherbound antique books, a bust on a pedestal base. Add a lamp, if there's an outlet nearby.

Mix in two or three small beloved objects: a tortoiseshell box, for example, or a pair of porcelain bud vases.

Now hang a single large picture, or a grouping of smaller ones,

The genius of a console

above the table. Stand back and admire—you've just given a bare wall a major decorative role in the room.

ARCHITECTURAL HALL TABLE

Make a console or hall table from two corbels, the chunky, embellished wooden brackets traditionally used as supports for porch roofs. (They can be antiques from a salvage yard, or reproductions from a millwork catalog.) Have the corbels secured to the wall. Top with thick beveled glass from a glass supply store, or with a piece of wood that's been finished on three sides with molding. The result looks more authentic and architectural than catalog versions made with decorative shelf brackets.

Tip: *Make the top an inch thick, or nearly so, to keep it in proportion to the corbels.*

SLIPCOVER A TABLE

Washington, D.C., designer Barry Dixon designed a highly tailored treatment for a dining table that was not used every day: Instead of using a tablecloth, he had it professionally slipcovered with straight fitted sides. For sit-down dinners, the slipcover was removed; but as the table served mostly for buffets or display, the cover—which had the crisp look of a custom white suit—stayed on for weeks at a time. Any slipcover maker can do this simple job.

Tip: *One good dressmaker detail will upgrade the design even further. Consider welting along the bottom hem in a contrasting color, or corner pleats lined in a contrasting color or texture. For his client's table, Dixon used linen for the cover and silk to line the corner pleats. Canvas and damask would make a less costly but equally intriguing marriage.*

THE WELL-PLACED SHELF

To make any room look cohesive and well edited, have a carpenter construct low shelves along an entire wall, just to the height of the window sills. Ask for a recessed baseboard, or toekick, a detail borrowed from freestanding furniture. Incorporate a radiator cover if you need one. The top shelf, perhaps 10 to 14 inches deep, makes a generous display ledge—much like an extended windowsill. Lower shelves will marshal books and other objects into instant organization.

You can also make the unit function as a window seat by deepening it to about 16 or 18 inches. To make sure the width and scale are what you want, make a pattern from newsprint and place it on the floor.

Tip: *Have holes drilled through the shelves in strategic locations, so the plugs of lamps or air conditioners can be slipped through, and plan cutouts as needed around electrical outlets. Make sure that any section covering the radiator can be easily opened.*

The well-placed shelf

ORNAMENTAL BOOKSHELF SUPPORTS

The most common kind of inexpensive shelving consists of standards and brackets, but those can have a telltale hardware-store look. There's an elegant alternative that won't drive up your budget: Buy shapely wooden brackets (sold precut at lumberyards and home decorating stores). They affix directly to the wall and can be painted the same color as the shelves they support.

Here's a no-sag formula from *At Home with Books* by Estelle Ellis and Caroline Seebohm (Clarkson Potter Publishers): An inch-thick shelf can go three feet between supports. If it must run longer, increase the thickness to 1-1/8 or 1-1/4 inches.

TELLTALE TRACKS

Built-in bookshelves and even store-bought units will look twice as expensive if the shelves are fixed in place—with no metal tracks or adjustable pegs running down the inside. Measure your tallest and shortest books or collectibles, then design or buy shelving that you know will accommodate them.

THE HIDDEN HINGE

Good custom shelving is often designed with a base of deep cabinets and open bookshelves above. One important detail to request: hinges placed *inside* the cabinet doors. It makes for a sleeker, more finished look.

SHELVES AND SEATING: AN INTIMATE FIT

If you are building in an entire wall of shelving, consider leaving an empty spot in the middle for a love seat or sofa. The love seat will feel nested in its space, creating a particularly cozy spot to sit. Leave three to four feet of wall space above the back of the sofa, partly so there's room to hang a picture or install a pair of small wall-

Shelves and seating: an intimate fit

mounted reading lights, and partly so that guests won't worry about banging their heads as they rise.

BOOKSHELVES WITH AN ENGLISH ACCENT

In a traditional English home, prints and paintings are hung directly over built-in bookshelves, as the added layers of decoration make a room look exceptionally rich. (Of course, you may have to move your great aunt's portrait in order to pull out the atlas.)

Bookshelves with an English accent

Shelves must be made of wood and run wall-to-wall, or at least neatly fill a niche, for this to work. Here's the recipe:

Mix a few vases or pieces of sculpture in with the books to avoid monotony. Alternatively, stack books on their sides at intervals along the shelves. It's a minor detail, but it creates a richer backdrop.

Choose older prints or paintings to hang on the shelves. Because the backdrop is busy with pattern and color, keep the subject matter of the pictures fairly straightforward—portraits, architectural drawings, and botanical prints are all good candidates. Hang the pictures directly from the vertical supports of the shelves, roughly at eye level.

Now, place a small table up against the shelves, preferably under one of the larger pictures. Top with candlesticks, flowers, and a book or two.

HALF SOFA, HALF BED

To give your bedroom the slightly distinguished look of a library or study, buy a sleigh bed, new or antique, and push it sideways against the wall. It will now resemble an overscaled sofa with shapely arms, giving the room a new elegance—and, perhaps just as important, more available floor space. A double or full-size bed, at 54 inches wide, will look far more lithe than a 60-inch-wide queen.

Tip: *For a finished look, use tailored (not ruffled) sham cases. They cost more than ordinary pillowcases, but don't have that sleepy domestic look. During the day dress the bed with oversize throw pillows and a deliciously textured shawl.*

NEW USES FOR ANTIQUE ÉTAGÈRES

The old-fashioned étagère, or display cabinet—tall, square, and open on all sides—brings a domestic look, not to mention great organization, to the home office. Stack your fax, printer, and reference books on the shelves, suggests design writer Carol Prisant. If your home office is also a bedroom or dining room, the étagère will soften its high-tech edges.

THE ROMANTIC BED

Buy mosquito netting at a home decorating store (roughly $50). It comes suspended from a wooden ring about the size of a dinner plate, and when you suspend the ring from a hook in the ceiling, yards and yards of translucent white netting fall like a veil around the bed. It's a very ethereal look, at a most down-to-earth price.

New uses for antique étagères

THE SPACE-SAVING GUEST BED

Remember that sleeper sofas come in love seat sizes, not just as lanky sofas. If you have a small living room, or one that must do double duty for dining or work, a love seat may free up some badly needed floor space.

THE STATUESQUE BED

Curiously, a tall four-poster bed can make a small bedroom look and feel larger. There are three reasons for this surprising effect: First, a four-poster bed won't block your view of the room, as the posts take up little air space. Second, your mind's eye assumes that any room containing so statuesque an object must be bigger than it looks. Third, the bed creates a strong focal point that distracts from the size of the space.

Tip: *It's best to avoid bed hangings, because in blocking your view, they'll psychologically shrink the space. If you really want bed curtains, make them sheer and very spare.*

SENSUAL SEATING

The most luxurious piece of furniture in the bedroom is not necessarily the bed. It's often a chaise longue, an inviting place to lean back, put up your feet, and read. Add a small table or low shelving nearby for books, a pillow, a telephone, and a throw for cold after-

noons. Aside from adding comfort, a chaise makes your bedroom versatile by turning it into a private living room.

Tip: *Angle the chaise out into the room—it may wilt, or lose its character, if it's up against the wall.*

GUEST QUARTERS

If you have an entire room devoted to guests, make it as flexible as possible: Buy two matching twin beds on casters, and keep two sizes of sheets—twin, for when the beds are rolled to opposite sides of the room, and king, for when they are pushed together.

Tip: *Twin-size trundle beds may not wheel easily around the room, but they will allow you to sleep four instead of two.*

BEDROOM SEATING

Less romantic than a chaise longue, but far more versatile, is an armchair-and-ottoman combination. The ottoman can be borrowed for extra seating in another room, or trundled under a writing desk when not in use.

NEXT TO THE BED

Don't bother with traditional nightstands in a small bedroom; they take up unnecessary space. Instead, make a low-profile bureau do double duty next to the bed, allotting part of the top drawer for personal items that the nightstand once held. Two tips to enhance a bedroom's sense of airiness: Use a bureau with legs, not one whose drawers begin at the floor; and if your walls are light in color, paint the bureau to match (assuming it's not a good antique). Lack of contrast between walls and furnishings can make a room look bigger.

THE ARTISTIC HEADBOARD

If you love the idea of commissioning a personal artwork, hire a decorative artist to design and paint a headboard onto a piece of wood that you affix to the wall. The headboard could incorporate motifs you love, such as cherubs or trellis, or it might be a trompe l'oeil mural of a Greek temple, with fragmented columns and a pediment. Though this is an investment because of the labor involved, you'll end up with a unique piece of art and a dramatic focal point for the room.

Tip: Make sure the artist seals the painting, so you can lean your head against it.

DISGUISING A FILE CABINET

If you have a home office in your bedroom, camouflage a filing cabinet as a bedside table. Here's how:

First, measure the distance between two *diagonal* corners of the cabinet. Add a half-inch to the measurement, and have a circle of inexpensive, quarter-inch plywood cut to that diameter.

Put the plywood top on the cabinet. Cover with a long flowing table skirt. Finally, top the fabric with a circle of glass (a half-inch thick, with a half-inch bevel), or for even more sparkle, use mirror (a quarter-inch thick, with a half-inch bevel). True, you have to lift up the fabric when you want access to your files. But you no longer have to share your bedroom with an ungainly metal cabinet.

A HEADBOARD FROM THE GARDEN

Buy a length of all-wood picket fencing, roughly 2 feet high. Give it a fresh coat of pure white paint, and affix it to the wall directly above your mattress.

BEDROOM LUXURY

One grace note you'll see in many beautiful bedrooms is an upholstered bench at the foot of the bed. To copy this look inexpensively, find a bench at a thrift shop or flea market, and recover it with new fabric, using a staple gun. (If it were living-room seating, you would have it professionally reupholstered, but the job of this bench is simply to look decorative.) Trim the edges with upholstery tacks (from any good fabric shop) if desired.

THE PAPER HEADBOARD

For a pared-down headboard, buy a single roll of a gorgeous, perhaps handpainted wallpaper. You'll need a piece at least 24 to 36 inches high, or taller if desired, and as wide as the bed; to get it, you may have to align several pieces or run the paper sideways. Affix the paper to the wall directly above the mattress, in precisely the space that a headboard would take up. (Frame with a wallpaper border if desired.) Now, order a piece of Plexiglas cut to the same dimensions from a lumberyard, a good hardware store, or a Plexiglas supplier. Screw it to the wall so that it covers the paper.

Tip: *Use gold-colored screws for a more polished look. Also: Ask your supplier to drill the holes in the Plexiglas for you.*

The paper headboard

CHAPTER 6

The Art of Display

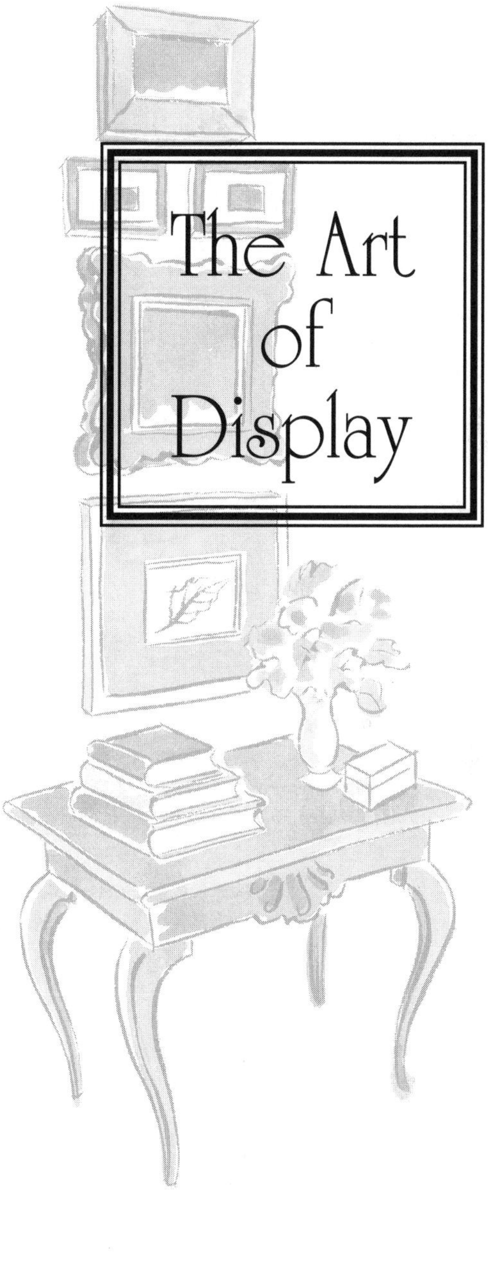

Lots of rules govern the display of beautiful objects, and frankly I'm grateful for them. They make decorating easier. Following (or even varying) these basic formulas can make your rooms look more confident, your taste more refined.

One of the most reassuring tricks of the trade is to mix truly good objects with lowborn ones: You can almost see the elegance rub off. New York designer Charlotte Moss applied this principle to a sitting room she created for the prestigious Kips Bay show house. She placed antique Japanese vases, each quite valuable, on the mantelpiece—then added simple white vases purchased at a Pier 1 store for $4.99 apiece. Suddenly the white porcelain stood out for its clean lines and curves, and the whole collection seemed to swell with importance. "When you put them all together, they find a way of relating to one another—and it's not by cost," says Moss. Rather, it's by line, by color, or by spirit, all of which matter far more for our living rooms than pedigree.

To pull this off, make sure that the objects somehow click with each other, and that each one, however plain or primitive, is beautiful in its own right. The late designer Billy Baldwin once found himself enchanted by the relationship between a pretty but ordinary lacquer box and a small painting by Renoir that was sited nearby. "If both the expensive and the inexpensive are, in their ways, first class," he wrote, "they can be perfectly harmonious."

THE MIRRORED GALLERY

To break the monotony of a long hallway and give it more character, hang a large collection of mirrors in beautiful old frames. They will create their own interior views, distracting from the narrowness of the space. Start with at least three or four mirrors along one wall, and add to the grouping as your collection grows. Hang the small ones stacked, two or three high; and align the whole grouping along the bottom, so the various tops form a kind of skyline.

Tip: *Look for slightly damaged but still-gorgeous frames at flea markets. Remove the picture, if there is one, and have a framer install a beveled mirror. You'll pay extra for the beveling, but it will make the mirror and frame look older and significantly more valuable.*

A GLIMPSE IN PASSING

If you have a small picture that gives you great pleasure, hang it at eye level right next to a doorway. It will give you an emotional lift every time you pass by.

COLLECTIBLES FROM THE CLOSET

Semiantique clothing from the local thrift shop can look exotic on the wall, and it's inexpensive to collect. Consider: a clutch of ladies' hats from the 1940s, complete with feathers and delicate veils; a pair of elegant beaded dresses; a grouping of vintage evening bags. Emily Mavrogenes, a Laura Ashley home stylist in Miami, suggests framing bits of antique lace, needlepoint, or crewel and grouping the frames on the wall. In a quirkier vein, Carol Olten, an interior designer in La Jolla, California, collects vintage gloves and drapes them languidly over her mantel and other furnishings.

UNEXPECTED ART

Not everything that hangs on your walls has to be rectangular, framed, and classifiable as art. Look for architectural or decorative elements with a form or surface that intrigues you, suggests Emily Mavrogenes. Among the possibilities: panes of leaded or colored glass, an antique kimono, a pair of weatherbeaten old shutters, carved wooden embellishments designed to hang over doorways, a piece of iron fencing, or huge letters from an old storefront or tavern sign.

Tip: *To enhance the status of something salvaged, hang it where fine art is conventionally displayed—over the fireplace, for example, or above the sofa.*

Unexpected art

CREATE HIERARCHY AMONG PHOTOGRAPHS

It's hard to linger over a collection of personal photographs on a tabletop when they all clamor equally for attention. To make a few of them standouts, put one or two photos into overscaled (up to 11-by-14-inch) mats and frames, which can either lean at the back of the grouping or hang slightly above it.

ENNOBLE A CHILD'S ARTWORK

Affixed to the refrigerator door, a child's paintings may have little esthetic value. But placed in another context, some of these early efforts can look like good modern art. To elevate your child's drawings or paintings into a meaningful collection, choose three or four pictures (an excellent number for a grouping), and have them professionally matted and framed, perhaps in simple black, silver, or gold wood. (Metal can look a bit cut-rate.) The pictures will appear striking and modern, visitors may not guess that the artist was underage, and your children will be intensely proud.

Tip: *The collection will look more cohesive if the frames match.*

Ennoble a child's artwork

VARY THE ALTITUDES

Objects on a mantel should be of varying heights; you want a skyline, not a level assemblage. Raise a few small objects, such as framed photos or ivory carvings, above their neighbors by creating pedestals that become part of the display: a stack of three leather-bound books, a pocket watch holder, an antique tortoiseshell box.

THE ART OF GROUPING PICTURES

Before you arrange pictures on a wall, group them into a rectangle or a square on the floor. First determine where the corners will go; then fill in the rest of the arrangement so that either the top or the bottom lines up neatly. (Both can be straight, but it's not essential.) Not every picture must conform perfectly to the outline of the rectangle, but the overall shape should be clear.

Now, give the arrangement some time to evolve. If it's at all complex, plan to step over the pictures for several days while you fine-tune the relationships between them. Then, and only then, should you transfer the dimensions of the large overall rectangle to the wall (by penciling in the corner marks) and start hammering in picture hooks.

Tip: *To keep plaster from crumbling as you hammer, put a piece of Scotch tape where the nail for the picture hook will go. If the picture is heavy, weigh it and ask a frame store for advice.*

CLASSIC ARRANGEMENTS

Some formulas for hanging art always seem to work:

Horizontal pairs. A pair of pictures—two nineteenth-century engravings, or two posters from the Peking Opera—can hang peaceably side by side; the arrangement will look balanced and

Classic arrangements

harmonious. If they are framed identically or at least similarly, they will be perceived as a matched set.

Stacked pairs. Any two pictures that look good together but differ in size can hang one over the other, usually with the smaller on top. This arrangement is a safer bet than trying to hang each picture solo, as it can look lonely or awkwardly placed.

Trios. Groupings of three always satisfy the eye. If the pictures are similar, they can be stacked in a narrow space or hung in a row. Either way, allow 1 or 2 inches between them for breathing space.

Quartets. A two-over-two arrangement looks quite impressive if the pictures are related. Four botanical prints or related photographs can be hung this way in any setting.

A COLLECTION OF CANDLESTICKS

If your dining-room centerpiece consists of two candlesticks flanking a flower arrangement, it's time to drag it out of the 1950s. Try grouping a large cluster of candlesticks in the center of the table. Mix crystal, glass, and metal; this isn't a Tiffany display but something highly personal.

Tip: *Use candles of different heights but all one color, so as not to detract from the candlesticks. You can never go wrong with white, cream-colored, or beeswax tapers.*

A collection of candlesticks

LET ONE IMAGE REIGN

A focal point is important not only to a room but to a constellation of pictures on a wall. If you're drawing dissimilar pictures into a single orbit, let one predominate so it draws the eye immediately into the arrangement. Of course, you don't want it to overwhelm its neighbors; experiment with different groupings, and trust your eye.

UPON AWAKENING

Display something you love—a collection of antique plates or a painting—on the wall opposite your bed. That way, the first thing you see in the morning will be an object that brings you pleasure.

REFLECT THE ARCHITECTURE

Try hanging small mirrors *above* eye level—poised over small paintings or watercolors, perhaps. Position the mirrors to reflect windows, interesting corners, or parts of the ceiling, so they enlarge your view of the room.

CHECK THE REFLECTION

Hanging a mirror is not unlike framing a view, which means that you must be conscious of what's reflected. Before driving in the nail, have a friend hold the mirror in position while you glance at it from a few key spots—the entry to the room, for example, and the sofa. Make sure that guests in the living room won't be staring at a reflection of the kitchen's stacked dishes, or an unmade bed.

RETHINKING THE COUNTRY BASKET

Baskets can be decorating clichés, but if you love them, study how professionals display them. A basket (whether straw or wire) is a sign of bounty and should *always* be overflowing—with soaps, cherry tomatoes, apples, lemons, magazines, bedside books, loose photographs, pinecones, nuts, dried roses, or garlic. When the supply starts to dwindle, refill the basket, or you'll lose that all-important look of abundance.

LIGHT A SPARK IN COLORED GLASS

Display colored bottles and glasses—especially vintage ones in cobalt, emerald, or ruby—on glass shelves set into the frame of a window. The sun will perform prismatic tricks with the tinted glass.

And curtains can hang in front of the shelves. (Shades, though, aren't compatible.)

__Tip:__ The shelves will be nearly invisible if you line them up with the mullions of the window.

FOCUS ATTENTION ON A NICHE

If you have a niche (a recess in the wall), fill it with built-in shelves; it's a marvelous chance to display books and objects. To emphasize the display, paint the entire niche (and if you like, the shelves) a color you love, or in a lighter or darker version of the wall color, so that it forms a rich backdrop.

__Tip:__ Be aware of how the backdrop color and the objects will interact. Then trust your personal preferences. White pitchers will pop out against a colored wall but will look sensual and more delicate against a white one. Bright Fiestaware stands out better against white, but if you paint the wall behind it aquamarine, the effect can be bold and gorgeous.

RE-CREATING THE HEARTH

If you don't have a fireplace, evoke the drama of one by installing a decorative mantel, or simply a mantel-height shelf on decorative brackets, and crowding it with candlesticks. Mix votive candles with beeswax pillars, crystal candlesticks with carved wooden ones. Collect until you have a serious congregation. Then take a long match and light the wicks. The flicker will be warm and riveting.

UPDATE THE GENTEEL BOTANICAL

Here's a fresh treatment for a set of old botanical prints, created by designer David H. Mitchell for *American HomeStyle & Gardening* magazine: Put the prints in fresh white mats (or use without mats, if you prefer), and have your framer sandwich them between panes of glass, held together with clips. All traces of fustiness will disappear, and the prints will look renewed.

A DIMINUTIVE EASEL

The little ebony-colored stands that usually display plates are also good for holding small picture frames. This is a good way to bring a variety of altitudes to a tabletop collection of family photographs and create a few focal points in a large arrangement.

UP ON A LEDGE

Decorative ledges—lengths of architectural molding up to 4 feet long—are sold mail-order by a number of companies, including Ballard, Spiegel, and Exposures (see "The Best Mail-Order Resources," Appendix B). Once a ledge is installed, it supports framed pictures or photographs that lean casually against the wall.

Among the advantages of a ledge: It gives the pictures prominence; it allows you to rotate your art, gallery style; it draws disparate objects into an instant collection; and it lets you instantly

Up on a ledge

undo any combinations that don't please you. Ledges can be stacked on the wall like shelves, three or four high, or run down the length of a hall.

Tip: *Keep the ledge itself fairly neutral—white, black, natural wood, or metal—to give the artwork center stage.*

FLAUNTING PORCELAIN

Collections of old Staffordshire or vintage plates and pitchers look terrific on the wall. For a classic display, buy an ornamental bracket of plaster or wood, and set a pitcher or bowl upon it. Then surround it with plates arranged in a diamond or circular shape. The plates create a frame for the pitcher, and the bracket adds an unexpected degree of depth.

EYE LEVEL

The best way to hang a picture is so your gaze meets it dead center or two-thirds of the way up the canvas. Try lowering it a few inches if it will hang in the living or dining room (where people will see it from a seated position), or if another picture will hang above it.

THE PORTRAIT GALLERY

Devote a single surface, such as a tabletop or bureau top, to small picture frames holding personal photographs. Decide early on whether you will collect frames of all kinds, creating an eclectic and highly personal group, or mix just two or three types of frames together—such as silver and marquetry—for a richer look.

Tip: *These are family photos, not works of art.*
Don't be afraid of overcrowding; it adds to the sense of warmth.

DINING-ROOM DISPLAY

Elsie de Wolfe, the famous American decorator, once said that the best principle of decorating was "Suitability! Suitability! Suitability!" And what could be more suitable for the walls of a dining room than a traditional plate rack? A simple wooden rack can cost as little as $50 (antique ones run in the hundreds) and can be stocked with patterned or all-white plates. Take them down for dinner; return them for display.

Tip: *Your plates don't have to match, but the display will have more graphic appeal if they are similar in pattern or color.*

INSTANT ART COLLECTION

T. Keller Donovan, a New York interior designer, found an inexpensive way to instantly gather an art collection for a young client: He bought a coffee table book of stunning flower photographs, cut the pages out with a razor blade, and had them inexpensively, identically framed in black, with pristine white mats. To make them look doubly impressive, he had the mats made overscale, with a 4-inch border all around. Finally, he hung the pictures in quartets, two over two, throughout the apartment—over the sofa, behind the dining table, and in other focal points.

Tip: *To make the collection look reasonably authentic, avoid pictures that are recognizable as copies, such as reproductions of Renoir paintings. For exquisite full-page flower photographs, try* The World Wildlife Book of Orchids *by Jack Kramer (Abbeville Press); for animals, I like the watercolors in* Trout: An Illustrated History *by James Prosek (Alfred A. Knopf).*

THE HIGH-IMPACT FRAME

To achieve the big bold gallery look when matting a picture, T. Keller Donovan always makes the mat larger than the norm—and even bigger along the bottom. An overscaled 4-inch border on the sides and top, for example, would call for a 4 1/2-inch border along the bottom. Some framers do this automatically, but if you are cutting your own mats or dealing with a new framer, it's a good formula to know. "There's a bit of an optical illusion involved," says Donovan, "and the bottom needs that extra bit in order to look equal all around."

OLD-FASHIONED ORGANIZERS

If the top of your dresser is overcrowded with photographs, perfume, and jewelry, buy a handful of lovely vintage ceramic dishes—saucers, small platters, even a delicate antique teacup to hold stray earrings—and use them to restore order. (You might pay $5 at a flea market for a Blue Willow dessert plate, or $15 for a small platter with a tiny chip; no need to get fancier than that.) The implication will be that you're well stocked with antique dishes and not afraid to scatter them through the house for daily use.

Tip: *Stick to one color or family of colors in collecting flea market ceramics—blue and white is a classic combination. Deploy a few in the bath, too, for makeup and soaps.*

LINE THE WALLS WITH ORIGINAL PHOTOGRAPHY

In the Dust Bowl years of the 1930s, master photographers like Dorothea Lange and Walker Evans began traveling the country, capturing images of hardship. They took thousands of pictures—portraits of people, houses, farm scenes, and scores of other subjects—under the Farm Security Administration (FSA) Photography Project, and the originals are quite valuable: One Lange print sold for $44,000 at auction.

What most people don't realize is that *anyone* can have an FSA photograph printed at a ridiculously low cost. An 11-by-14-inch exhibition-quality black and white print is just $45. (Glossies are $12 but won't look professional.) You can assemble a moving and authentic collection this way, particularly if the photos you choose are related in theme or spirit.

The closest thing to a catalog is the book *Documenting America, 1935–1943*, by Carl Fleischhauer and Beverly Brannan (University of California Press, 1988; paperback, $30). Order it through bookstores, or call the publisher at (510) 642-4247. Alternatively, check a library for the out-of-print *A Vision Shared* by Hank O'Neal (St. Martin's Press, 1976). Both books provide the negative numbers that you'll need for ordering prints.

Write: Library of Congress, Photoduplication Service, Washington, D.C. 20540. Request an order form for photographic prints, a price list, and information on the FSA photographs.

PICTURES IN THE ATTIC

How do you hang pictures in an attic bedroom, where the walls slope? This technique comes from design writer Carol Prisant:

- In each of the frame's two top corners, affix a small metal triangular picture mount (sold at hardware, houseware, and framing stores).
- In each of the frame's two bottom corners, insert a short

screw that won't break through the front of the frame. Don't screw it all the way in.

- To the wall, affix two standard picture hooks where you want the two top corners of the frame to go. Hang the picture from these hooks, holding it flat against the wall with your hand. Make two pencil marks to indicate where the bottom-most screws touch the wall. Remove the picture.
- Insert two more screws into the wall where you've made the marks. Screw these most of the way in, but not all the way.
- Hang the picture again, holding it flat against the wall.
- Take a 6-inch length of picture wire. Wrap one end around the exposed neck of a wall screw until it's secure. Now wrap the rest of the wire around the screw on the picture. As you wind it, you'll be reeling the picture in until the wire is tight and the picture touches the wall. Cut off any leftover wire. Repeat with the second screw.

THE BRACKETED OBJECT

Decorative brackets—ornamental supports that affix to a wall and hold a single object—are excellent for display. Brackets can be used singly, hung in pairs, or massed together. They let you show off three-dimensional objects such as vases or pitchers without having to install shelves. And, of course, you can rotate your collectibles in and out of view.

__Tip:__ If you are displaying items that are virtually identical, like a pair of sculptural pitchers, the brackets don't have to match. But if the objects differ, says designer Barbara Southerland, keep the brackets identical.

THE CAMERA: A SECOND OPINION

To turn what Carol Prisant calls "a shockingly objective eye" on any arrangement—art, collectibles, furnishings—take a photograph. The camera may reveal problems and solutions that weren't apparent before.

CLIMBING THE STAIRS

A collection of related pictures can literally zigzag up a staircase. Simply make sure that each picture is hung at eye level and that the spacing between them is kept constant.

DISPLAY SHELF

For a collection of similar objects, such as handcrafted birdhouses or art deco vases, install a long wooden shelf about 18 to 24 inches below the ceiling. Run the shelf across an entire wall, making sure it looks finished from underneath. (You can make a narrow room look wider by running the shelf along one of the short walls.) Arrange objects with ample breathing space between them, so that your eye can linger over each one in turn.

Tip: *To determine the best height for your shelf, ask a friend to hold a piece of wood at different heights, and mark the spot you choose. If the wall is windowed, you may want to run the shelf just above the top of the window frames.*

FORGOTTEN SPACES

If you have two or three similar small pictures, try hanging them in a row over a door or under a window. Because the placement is so unexpected, the pictures will draw extra attention.

SUGGESTED READING

Decorating with Pictures by Stephanie Hoppen (Clarkson Potter Publishers) dwells on framing, matting, and arranging, all quite helpfully.

Forgotten spaces

CHAPTER ◆ 7

Telling Details

Details are your decorating signature. A detail can be an accessory, like a lamp or a Venetian glass bowl; or it can be a finishing touch, like the moss fringe on a pillow. Happily, details are usually easy to decide on, or at least to experiment with. It's hard to make an egregious mistake with something like a candlestick or a vase.

Though small, details can also be the richest elements in a room. For example, if you salvage a tight budget by slipcovering a sofa in plain cotton duck, you can still telegraph luxury by investing in two stunning throw pillows—oversize, down-stuffed, and covered with velvet or damask or silk, perhaps in the same color as the cotton duck. The fabric may cost $50 or $100 a yard, but one yard may be enough—and your canvas sofa will take on a new and unexpected opulence.

Finally, details may keep you happy until you can afford larger improvements. For example, I can't yet spring for a four-poster bed, or an apartment with a separate study; as a result, my bed sits on a metal frame and shares space with a desk and files. But narcissus bulbs are sprouting in blue-willow eggcups, probably from the 1920s; the switchplate is dark green ceramic, with leafy imprints; and the bed linens are an orchid print in red and cream. Simply because I adore them, these touches make up for a lot of decorating sins.

Some details, such as lampshades, live or die by quality. Others, like the uplights we hide behind plants, don't. Over time, if you look at enough details you think are fantastic and also at those you dislike, you'll develop your own sense of which ones require investment and which don't.

Most important, details are your chance to indulge. You may have to agonize over paint colors or deliberate for days over the choice of a sofa. But if you fall in love with a lone candlestick at a flea market, why on earth should you hold back?

ONE MAGNIFICENT BOWL

If there is such a thing as the perfect accessory, it is probably the footed bowl. This simple object is simply a glass or ceramic bowl that grows out of a pedestal, rather like a cake stand. Rima Suqi, a New York stylist and design writer, often uses one in photo shoots.

One magnificent bowl

"A footed bowl rises above everything around it," she says. And as a serving piece, of course, it dramatizes the food.

Tip: *Lemons are great for heaping into a glass bowl. Use them fresh for inexpensive and long-lasting color, or dry them in strong sunlight. To do this, line up lemons on a south-facing windowsill and rotate them every few days. The lemons will darken to orange and, when totally dry, take on a rough, almost walnutlike texture. A faint citrus scent will cling to them for at least a year.*

REPEAT A SYMBOL

If you are fond of a particular motif—perhaps leaves, vines, or roses—use it to unify your decorating choices throughout your home. You might find leaves, for example, in fabrics, old majolica plates, rugs, embossed towels, placemats, and botanical prints. Repeating this kind of accent from one room to the next is a subtle but superb way to harmonize.

ASIATIC GRACE NOTES

Stir a decorative lacquered bowl or box into any room that needs a bit of polish—a tip borrowed from Billy Baldwin. From coromandel screens to simple Japanese boxes, lacquer brought warmth and charm to his rooms. "It is at home anywhere," he once wrote, "at ease in a palace, never too proud to be in a cottage."

THE IMPORTANCE OF FRESH FLOWERS

The editors of top design magazines won't let a room be photographed until a spray of fresh flowers has been added. Among the photo stylists' tricks:

- Cut roses short, and crowd them into a silver cup or some other pretty short container. Because everyone expects to see long-stemmed roses bristling from a vase, yours will stand out for their informality, and look freshly picked as well.

The importance of fresh flowers

- Collect miniature vases or bottles, put two or three blossoms in each, and line them up in front of a window.
- Arrange large bouquets or branches in a silver-plated champagne bucket. New York designer William Sofield did this with sunflowers, which he first plucked clean of their yellow petals—leaving the velvety-black centers surrounded by spiky green leaves.
- Heap hydrangeas (no vase necessary) on top of a tall piece of furniture, such as a bookshelf or armoire, so they spill slightly over the top. The hydrangeas will dry in place, creating a lovely, delicate froth of flowers and more than a hint of nostalgia.
- Look for unorthodox containers. A personal favorite: large (28-oz.) cans of Sclafani crushed tomatoes, with a picture of bright red plum tomatoes printed directly on the metal.
- Buy sprays of greenery—eucalyptus, box, beargrass, or anything else that strikes you—and add just a few long-stemmed flowers for color. This will keep your weekly flower costs down.

Tip: *To prolong the life of flowers, use only vases that have been scrupulously scrubbed. To keep bacteria from breeding around the flower stems, stir in one teaspoon of bleach per gallon of water.*

DECORATIVE DRAWERS

Knobs on cabinets and bureaus can serve as jewelry for a room if you change standard hardware to sculptural fittings. Knobs and pulls can be found in the shapes of shells, twigs, knives, forks, fruit, and Greek columns. You're more likely to find these in artistic home decorating stores or even in catalogs (see "The Best Mail-Order Resources," Appendix B) than in a local hardware store.

***Tip:** For kitchen cabinets, bring an old pull when you shop to make sure the new ones will fit the same holes.*

THE MAGNIFICENT THROW PILLOW

If you can't afford an extravagant silk or damask for your sofa, indulge in a yard or two for throw pillows. You'll be amazed at the way a few great pillows can telegraph opulence through an entire room.

Recipe for a designer-quality throw pillow:

- Make it overscaled (20 to 28 inches square)
- Stuff with an economical 50–50 or 95–5 mix of feathers and down (cheaper than 100 percent down, which designers prefer, but infinitely more plush than foam). Pillow forms in

The magnificent throw pillow

many sizes can often be found, well priced and ready-made, at large fabric stores like Calico Corners.

- Edge with dressmaker detailing—fat welting (the cording around a pillow's edge), or a flange, or moss fringe, a thick and bushy trim. Unless you can sew your own welting, have an upholsterer make your pillows; it may cost $50 to $75, but you're buying big shots of confidence and glamour for the room.
- Have the pillow made with a hidden zipper for easy cleaning.

Tip: *Use two or three different fabrics for your various pillows; they need to match only in spirit, or in their sense of luxury. As for the little foam pillows that came with your sofa, put the fabric in storage (in case you ever need extra) and throw out the forms.*

THE NONTRADITIONAL TABLE SKIRT

Avoid predictability at dinner. Some alternatives to the usual store-bought tablecloth:

- Put a large square napkin under each plate. Turn the napkin diagonally so that one point spills over the edge of the table.
- Drape a table with two or three long runners that hang over the edges, so that pairs of guests who face each other will be using opposite ends of each runner as a placemat.
- Cover a round table with a large square tablecloth. The corners will gracefully drape into points.
- Have a floor-length skirt made for a small round table, and top the table with a half-inch-thick round of beveled glass. (If your table has rounded or bullnose edges, make sure the glass extends all the way to the end of the bullnose, or it will appear too small for the table.)

Initialize a room

INITIALIZE A ROOM

Monograms are standard on towels—but try them in the living room, where the unexpected context brings out their elegance. Buy a solid-colored fabric of substance, like velvet or heavy cotton, and have a huge monogram—perhaps 12 or 15 inches high—stitched in the middle in contrasting thread. (White thread on black fabric, purple on white—be as dramatic as you like.) Center the monogram on a throw pillow or on the front or back of an upholstered side chair.

Tip: *Monogrammers are listed, not surprisingly, under "Monograms" in the Yellow Pages. Some use computers; others have monogramming machines, and still others do the embroidery by hand. The method may affect the price—get two or three estimates if possible.*

DRESSED-UP BUREAUS

To offset simple porcelain or wooden knobs on a cabinet or chest, remove the knobs and affix a square of silver, copper, or composite gold leaf on the surface behind each one. (Leaf is sold at large art-supply stores.) Seal with nonyellowing clear varnish or water-based polyurethane. When you reattach the knobs, each will be framed by a gleaming metallic square.

Tip: *For an easy introduction to gilding, try your bookstore:* The Gilding Kit *by Glenn McDean (Watson Guptill) includes a handsome book on decorating with gold leaf* and *10 sheets of leaf.*

IRON BARS AND IVY

Apartment windows often have metal bars to keep children from leaning out. Wrap the bars with fake ivy—of fabric, not plastic—and secure with wire.

Tip: *Remove in winter, when it looks inappropriate.*

GRAPHIC DESIGN

In a contemporary interior, single out one architectural element, like a banister or exposed rafters, by painting it a striking color, such as red, eggplant, or teal.

DEMAND SUBSTANCE FROM DOORS

Replace hollow-core doors, which look flimsy from afar, with solid ones. Among the options: a French door with one tall pane of glass (line it with lace for privacy) or a plain door with panels suggested by molding, which a carpenter can apply. If you are renovating, you can buy an antique door from a salvage yard, and have a doorway rebuilt to fit around it.

Tip: *At the very least, upgrade your doors by changing the hardware, including hinges, to high-quality new or vintage pieces. Bring the old hardware with you so you can precisely match its fittings.*

WALLPAPER DECOUPAGE

Snip a beautiful motif from leftover wallpaper and decoupage it to a piece of wooden furniture—the top of a plain occasional table, or the back of a pair (or more) of dining chairs. As with all decoupage, seal with several coats of polyurethane.

NEW TERRITORY FOR RUGS

Richly colored flat-weave rugs, such as kilims and dhurries, can look particularly exotic when you take them off the floor.

- Drape a flat-weave rug over a dining or coffee table, and top with glass. If the table is round, consider draping it first with a floor-length circle or square of richly colored fabric. The rug will then serve as an overlayer of color.

- Have an upholsterer use the good sections of a worn antique rug as upholstery for throw pillows and ottomans. (Rugs can look good as chair upholstery, too, but consider the scratchiness factor.) With this use in mind, a $20 antique rug with holes can be a garage-sale steal.

THE UNOBTRUSIVE AIR CONDITIONER

Nothing interrupts a beautiful view (or highlights a bad one) as intrusively as a window air-conditioning unit. To make it less prominent, remove the entire front panel and spray-paint it, first with a primer, then with white paint. Then slide the air conditioner to one side of the window or the other, so it's no longer centered, and replace those plastic accordion side-panels with a single rectangle of clear Plexiglas. (A hardware store can usually cut one to your measurements for less than $10.) The Plexiglas will require weather-stripping around the edges, but the air conditioner will look much smaller and steal less of your view.

ROOM JEWELRY

When was the last time you looked at your switchplates? If they look tired or ordinary, go shopping for dressier ones. (Try a major lighting store, or a catalog such as Ballard.) Switchplates come in white, gold, silver, and mirror; some are flat, others elaborately carved or cast. You may even find some that are decoupaged with replicas of major paintings. Think of a switchplate as an earring for the room, and have some fun with it.

Tip: *Many lights, particularly halogen, belong on dimmers. Have the dimmer installed before you invest in a decorative switchplate, as it will determine the shape of the opening you need.*

THE SIMPLEST FIRESCREEN

Instead of buying an expensive handpainted firescreen to block the view of a barren hearth in winter, take a tip from Beverly McGuire, who produces design stories for top decorating magazines. She bought a length of short white picket fence whose pickets were connected with wire, not wood. (A roll cost $20 at a garden center.) Then she snipped off a length about 50 percent longer than the fireplace interior. She undulated the fencing into gentle curves so it would stand up by itself—being made with wire, it held the shape—and planted it just inside the empty fireplace. Even in winter it brought a touch of the garden indoors.

THE ROMANTIC CLOSET

Edge your closet shelves with lace trim from a fabric shop. (Secure it in place with white-topped thumbtacks.) The lace adds a moment of pleasure to such everyday acts as retrieving a clean towel.

The simplest firescreen

THE WHITE-LAMINATE FIX

White laminate shelving, often purchased as an inexpensive storage solution, may look out of place a few years later, as your rooms fill with better or older furnishings. To help her own laminate shelves blend in until she could replace them, design writer Terry Trucco edged them with black grosgrain ribbon of the same width as the shelves. Her technique: Have one person apply Magna-Tac 809 Adhesive (sold in fabric and craft stores) to a soft toothbrush and rub it along the edge of the shelf, while the second person follows behind and presses the ribbon into place. (The adhesive dries fast, hence the need for two people.)

Note that your books must be aligned with the front edge of the shelves, or too much laminate will show.

Tip: *For the name of a store that carries Magna-Tac, or to order it directly from the manufacturer, call (914) 699-3400.*

EDIT YOUR HOUSEPLANTS

A fringe of plants on the windowsill can look bedraggled. Worse, we tend to get attached to the stragglers, making it hard to weed them out. One option is to give the plants away and replace them with one or two statuesque trees—a braided ficus, a palm, or a rosemary topiary that rises in a spiky twist.

Alternatively, buy a plant stand with stepped shelves, and let it organize the collection of greenery into a grouping with more visual impact.

ARTISTIC SHADOWS

The beauty of a ficus or palm tree lies not just in the leaves but in the shadows they can cast. If you have this kind of tree in your home, buy an inexpensive uplight—a canister-shaped light that sits unobtrusively on the floor, shining upward—and position it behind the pot. (Not too close, or the hot bulb may wither the leaves.) The light will throw marvelous spiky shadows across the ceiling, adding instant drama to the room.

BRING BACK CANDLELIGHT

Add real romance to any room by hanging wall sconces that hold candles rather than electric bulbs. You can buy simple ones from catalogs such as Crate & Barrel (see "The Best Mail-Order Resources," Appendix B) and more ornate, gilded fixtures from auction houses or antique shops. The light will be soft and flickering, and the fixture will look entrancing even when the candles are out.

Tip: *Always burn a new candle for a minute or two before setting it into a sconce—or into any candleholder, for that matter. An unused candle looks like a prop.*

Bring back candlelight

ERASE A ROOM'S SHADOWS

If a room feels dreary, look up: Chances are it's lit solely by an incandescent fixture attached to the ceiling. But there are several ways to dispel the shadows that are causing the gloom:

- Buy a halogen torchère—a tall, standing lamp that aims its beam straight up—and turn it on every time you enter the room. The brighter, whiter halogen will mix with the standard incandescent light, and make the room infinitely more cheerful. A serviceable torchère can be found for less than $20 in black or white, slightly more in brass, through Staples, a mail-order catalog (see The "Best Mail-Order Resources," Appendix B). Keep halogen torchères away from all things flammable, especially curtains.
- Replace the overhead fixture with a ceiling-mounted halogen light, a simple job for an electrician. These handsome halogen fixtures can easily be found for about $100.
- Replace the overhead fixture with a ceiling fan. Not only is it pretty, but it will distribute heat and air conditioning more evenly throughout the room. (Do not buy a fan with lights attached, or you'll repeat the depressing effect.)

Pivotal design tip: *Torchères come with their own dimmers, but for ceiling fixtures, your electrician should install a rheostat or dimmer—an adjustable switch that will let you set the mood and brightness of the room from cheerful (full voltage) to romantic (dimmed). Don't skip this step; halogen is far too powerful to be limited to "on" and "off."*

Energy-saving tip: *A halogen bulb costs $8 to $10, but you can double its life by keeping it dimmed just 10 percent—the merest sliver of a turn on the dimmer. Once every week or so, however, you* must *turn the dimmer all the way up for a full minute, so the filament can renew itself.*

MAKING THE SILVER SHINE

For clients who entertain formally and frequently, Ann Kale has downlights recessed over the dining-room table. This requires some investment, as the downlights and their wiring must be installed by an electrician, and the ceiling will need repainting afterward. But nothing, not even a chandelier, can make crystal and silver sparkle like a few downlights overhead.

Tip: *Make sure the electrician installs* commercial-grade *downlights, in which the bulb is amply recessed to avoid glare. The alternative—residential quality—"is a fancy name for lower-grade fixtures," cautions Kale.*

POURING IN LIGHT

The best way to light a room with color-saturated walls is to keep the ceiling white and add a torchère or two, says New York lighting designer Ann Kale. A torchère will bounce light off the white ceiling; more than 80 percent of that light will be reflected back into the room.

THE ALL-AMERICAN LAMP

One of the most classic lamps in America is the brass swing-arm lamp, a fixture that Billy Baldwin used again and again in his interiors. Wall-mounted over a bed or sofa or sitting on a writing desk, it is sympathetic with every style of decorating. (It's also one of the easiest lamps to find at retail.) Thanks to its popularity, it's also affordable; if you find one on sale, you might pay as little as $39.

Tip: *To keep the electrical cord from snaking conspicuously down the wall, buy cord covers, either in brass to match the lamp or in white to match the walls. The more custom solution is also the more expensive: Have an electrician bury the wiring inside the wall.*

HOW TO DRESS A LAMP

Fitting a shade to a lamp base requires an expert eye, so yes, you must lug the base to a lampshade store. A few guidelines:

- The shade should come low enough to obscure the socket that holds the bulb.
- If the base is fancy, crown it with a plain shade; if the base is simple, you can use a more elaborate shade. If in doubt, you can never lose with a simple high-quality shade.
- Judge a shade by how it looks on the *illuminated* lamp.

- Buy a classic—white linen, parchment, or black linen. *White linen* is most translucent; use it when you want the lamp to help illuminate the whole room. (It's not good for bedtime reading lamps if one partner wants to sleep.) *Parchment* is slightly translucent; it transmits a low glow. *Black linen* allows little or no light to escape through the shade; it will illuminate the book on your lap but not the space around you.

A GENTLE RADIANCE

Have your lampshades professionally lined in pink or gold by a shade supplier. This designer detail stays in the background, but it works a low-key magic. The glow of light on gold conveys a quiet opulence; pink creates a soft cast that's particularly flattering to the complexion.

LAMP JEWELRY

Finials, those decorative little toppers that sit on top of lamps and hold the shades in place, should be chosen with the same sense of style—either gregariousness or restraint—that you bring to your own jewelry.

UPGRADE A SISAL RUG

With fabric glue, such as Magna-Tac 809 Adhesive, affix a length of wide grosgrain ribbon around the border of a sisal rug. (No, the ribbon can't be cleaned—but neither can sisal.) Alternatively, stencil a decorative flourish in the corners of the rug or along the edges.

Tip: *The best stenciling paint for sisal rugs, according to designer and* Metropolitan Home *columnist David Staskowski, is oil paint or artist's oils, slightly thinned with turpentine.*

THE GRACEFUL RADIATOR

Few things intrude on a design scheme more than an uncovered (or badly covered) radiator. But some designers will occasionally *bare* the radiator, giving it a fresh coat of white paint and acknowledging its sculptural presence. In summer, you can drape the radiator with a veil of sheer fabric that puddles on the floor and allows its bones to show through. Or consider topping the radiator with a wooden shelf held up by a decorative bracket on either side, and let the radiator be its slinky self underneath.

The graceful radiator

The caveat: Exposed radiators look best in simple rooms—white walls, high ceilings, uncluttered tabletops, and an overall mood of serenity.

Tip: *To paint a radiator, buy a radiator mitt at the paint store. Worn like a mitten, it lets you slather on the paint by hand and makes the job easier than a brush. Paint the radiator the same color as the wall.*

SPLIT-PERSONALITY PILLOWS

Make reversible pillows that can change the mood of your living room simply by being flipped back to front. On one side, for example, you might use white damask; it will give the room an elegant and slightly formal air. On the other side, you might have awning stripes or a garden chintz that reminds you of spring. Choose a neutral welting or fringe that works with both sides.

GREETING THE DAY

One of the first sights that greets you every morning is probably your alarm clock. Did you buy it at the drugstore ten years ago? Consider the clock, like so many other small accessories, a piece of jewelry for the room. Buy a new one that not only looks terrific but awakens you with a nice sound as well.

Do You Need an Interior Designer?

A designer can perceive the potential of our homes in ways that most of us can't. We aren't trained to. Nor do we attend to every little detail that surrounds us—something designers excel at. For me, this really sank in the day a designer named Carl D'Aquino came over bearing his portfolio, and sunflowers from the corner market. I thanked him, and took the flowers.

He took them back.

Flowers in hand, he walked into my kitchen, hunted down the shears, and began nosing around for a suitable container. I brought in a cobalt blue vase, which apparently pleased him, because he set it down and trimmed the sunflower stems. Then he checked them against the vase. Then he trimmed them again. Then, when the flowers were in water, he did something I can only describe as fluffing, the way my hair stylist does at the end of a cut. And the sunflowers? They looked more artistic, yet more wild, than any sunflowers *I* ever brought home.

If a designer can do this with flowers, imagine what he can do with an entire room.

Now, our rooms don't have to be perfect, any more than our flowers do. (Let's keep things in perspective here; this is decorating, not life.) But at some point you may long for expert guidance—perhaps when there are five test-swatches of yellow paint on the wall and you can't choose between them, or when your living room seems stiff no matter where you put the sofa.

If that time comes, there are several ways, all fairly affordable, to pick the brains of an interior designer. He or she won't "do" your entire home, but you *can* get professional advice about paint and wallpaper, furniture arrangements, lighting, whether to buy a new sofa or slipcover the old one, or where to squeeze in a home office—just about any specific question you can think of.

Among your choices:

HIRE A DESIGN SERVICE THAT DOES SAME-DAY MAKEOVERS

In a typical session, the designer will ask about your needs or concerns; make concrete suggestions for whatever needs attention most—color, window treatments, art, or accessories—and sketch a new floor plan for you to follow. In some cases, she'll mail you a list of suggestions, swatches, and sources after the consultation.

This works best when you have three or four very specific questions ready, listed, mentally or on paper, in order of importance. I recently hired a New York firm called Room Redux that charges $125 an hour, with a four-hour minimum, to visit a home, make specific suggestions, then write up a report complete with recommendations, paint swatches, and recommended sources for lighting, furniture, or whatever is needed. My first question was how to seat ten people in my living room, which then felt crowded with six. The Room Redux women actually helped rearrange my furniture on the spot—though this may go beyond the normal call of duty—and it looked terrific. My remaining questions, about a bedroom, a home office, and a complicated little hall also got answered.

Was everything perfect? Of course not. I chose a different color for the hall, in the end, and we disagreed on nightstands. But these short-term designers solved the biggest problem in our apartment, and gave us good sources and advice.

Same-day design services often advertise in city magazines and the home sections of newspapers. With names like Use What You Have Interiors or Rent A Decorator ("No job too small"), you can be reasonably sure they're not trying to draw you into an expensive, long-term relationship. If your questions are straightforward ("What color do I paint my walls?" "How do I arrange my bedroom furniture?"), this can be an ideal way to go.

Some questions to ask before you make an appointment:

- What do you charge? How much time does that cover? Is all of that time spent working with me in my home?
- How much is an extra hour or a follow-up visit, if I decide I want more time?

- Can you refer me to upholsterers, carpenters, or slipcover makers, if I need to have work done?
- Do you mail me a write-up of your ideas, or should I take notes?
- What advance preparation, if any, should I do before your visit?

ASK A TOP-OF-THE-LINE DESIGNER FOR A CONSULTATION ONLY

A very established designer may consider $50,000 a modest budget—for one room. But if you are stricken with the work of one of these stars, you may be able to afford a one-time consultation.

When you telephone, you'll probably end up talking with an assistant, but don't let that stop you. Name the magazines where you've seen the designer's work. Explain that you're smitten with her interiors but can't afford her. And ask if she ever does one-time consultations. If so, ask the cost.

Here's how it works: You get to consult with a major talent; she gives you concrete suggestions; and you carry them out yourself, with no one to hold your hand. Prices will vary in different cities, but in New York typical fees might range from $1,000 for two hours to $3,500 for a day.

Incidentally, if your designer of choice says no, don't stop there. Ask if she has trained any talented young designers whom she might recommend.

HIRE A DESIGNER BY THE HOUR, FOR A LIMITED TIME

By looking through magazines or asking friends for recommendations, settle on a designer whose work or personal style you like. Ask if she will meet with you for just a few hours, charging an hourly rate. (The hourly rate matters, because some designers make a profit only by marking up the furnishings they sell you—and you may not want to feel pressured to buy.)

For perhaps $100 an hour—that is, somewhere in the nationwide $75- to $250-an-hour range—you can easily engage a designer for three hours, or six, or whatever you need. This arrangement differs from a consultation because *you* decide when it's over, and because you can always call back for more guidance. For example, you might invest in four hours and divide them over two visits—the first for ideas that you carry out yourself, the second for visual polishing and accessorizing. Six months later, you might ask the designer back to discuss another room that you haven't yet tackled.

TEN WAYS TALK TO AN INTERIOR DESIGNER

1. Know what you like. Gather magazine photos into Love and Hate files. They're like shorthand to a designer—an instant handle on your taste.

2. Before you meet, ask what the designer charges, and be frank about what you can spend. You might say, for instance, "I can only afford four hours of your time at this

stage, and I have questions about color and furniture. What can we get done in that amount of time?"

3. Have three or four specific questions ready *before* you meet with the designer, and write them down in order of priority. That way, if you only get through half the list, it will be the important half.

4. Decide in advance whether you're hiring the designer just for advice or to help you shop for furnishings (or both). One woman engaged a designer for six hours and found herself agreeing to let the designer spend a couple of those hours shopping for a table. The designer tracked one down for about $4,000—not bad for a nice Italian antique. But the client, who had hoped to buy an old farm table at a country auction for less than $1,000, was taken aback. She paid for the time spent shopping, of course, but had nothing to show for it.

Ideally, the designer would have asked what her new client could spend on a table, and a more experienced client would have put a firm upper limit on the cost.

5. Assume that the first meeting will be held at your home, which the designer needs to see. You're not likely to be asked to meet at her office, but if you are, decline.

6. Ask the designer to bring her fan deck to the first meeting. A fan deck is a collection of paint swatches that

literally spreads out like a fan; with it, you can get started on choosing colors.

Don't be shocked if it doesn't appear. Designers know that a fan deck, with its hundreds of hues, can overwhelm some clients. Still, you may not want to pay for a second meeting just to go over paint colors. In this case, ask the designer to mail you swatches for your consideration after she's seen your home. Of course, if you don't love the colors she picks out, you may need a second meeting anyway. Color is highly personal, and choosing it often involves some trial and error.

7. When you meet, ask where you should invest your "serious" money and where you can economize. A designer can be terrific at helping you set priorities. For example, she may point out that any money you invest in a good antique Oriental rug can probably be recouped, while an expensive coffee table loses most of its value the minute you bring it home. She can also suggest a decorating timetable, if you have to parcel out your expenditures over several months or years.

8. Be frank about your likes and dislikes. It's one thing to murmur "How nice" when your grandmother gives you a sweater in an unfortunate hue. If a designer shows you the same color in a wallpaper sample, don't hedge—say "It's too bright" or "No, it's not me." The happiest client is always the one who spoke up.

9. If the designer suggests things you can't afford—a new sofa, built-in bookshelves, an Oriental rug—ask her these two questions:

- Can I save money by making any of these purchases at a flea market or consignment shop?
- Can you list the key purchases in order of importance, so I can make them over the next several years?

10. If your relationship is going to last longer than a few hours, ask for a contract or letter of agreement that spells out the job and the fees. As with any contract, read before you sign.

IS THERE A RISK IN HIRING A DESIGNER?

Sure.

Maybe you won't like her advice—the shade of gray she picked out for you is steely, not soft. Maybe she's trying to steer you into something you can't afford, either because she thinks it's perfect for you or because she's trying to draw you into a long-term and lucrative (for her) relationship. Maybe you feel uncomfortable rejecting her ideas face-to-face.

But because you're paying only for hours, not months, of her time, the downside is pretty small.

When I lived in Chicago, I hired a designer for two hours to suggest a shade of pale gray for the walls, to help me plan a checkerboard floor for the kitchen, and to help stage a guest room in my walk-in closet, the largest I had ever seen.

This designer's idea of a checkerboard was so asymmetrical, it set my teeth on edge, and every shade of gray she offered had a hardness to it, like metal. But she did save me from a huge costly disaster with the walk-in closet, which had no business being a guest room, and she suggested a better way to accommodate guests. To me, that was more than worth the $160 we paid.

If your brief role as a client doesn't work out, just draw from the experience whatever you can and try it again later with someone else. Design is a creative field, so no two designers will solve a problem the same way—in fact, it's amazing how much they can differ. Ultimately, expert advice, whether you cleave to it or not, tends to be a pretty good investment.

The Best Mail-Order Resources

Catalogs, used wisely, can sometimes save both time and money. A few suggestions for wise mail-order decorating:

- Don't furnish an entire room from one catalog, lest it look like an advertising set.
- Be wary of a company's signature items. If you can instantly tell that a particular oak desk comes from Levenger or a particular table from Pottery Barn, you may want to pass it up. Instead, look for items that strike you as unusual—or else so classic, they can't be pegged to a single source.
- If you can't see it in person, I don't rec-

ommend mail-ordering dark brown furniture with curvaceous Queen Anne legs—because so much of it looks like it's been stamped out by the same machine. The same thing goes for low-cost country pine.

- Frames are one thing, but don't buy framed pictures from catalogs. Art is not a decorator accessory.
- Unless you know the products or completely trust the source, don't buy a sofa or easy chair you haven't test-driven for comfort.

What follows is a listing of interesting catalogs. Most are free or inexpensive; costlier ones are noted.

Art & Artifact
2451 East Enterprise Parkway
Twinsburg, OH 44087
(800) 231-6766

Exotic and semiantique-looking home accessories, small furnishings, and statuary.

Ballard Designs
1670 DeFoor Avenue, N.W.
Atlanta, GA 30318-7528
(404) 351-5099

A rich mix of furnishings and accessories: chandeliers and sconces, tables, urns, botanical prints, display shelves, even a leopard-print Louis XV–style armchair.

Bloomingdale's by Mail
475 Knotter Drive
Cheshire, CT 06410-1130
(800) 777-0000

Designer towels and sheets; an assortment of furniture.

The Bombay Company
P.O. Box 161009
Fort Worth, TX 76161
(800) 829-7789

Console tables, coffee tables, mirrors, ceramics, and more.

Chambers
P.O. Box 7841
San Francisco, CA 94120-7841
(800) 334-9790

Upscale bedding, including the beds; bath linens, expensive soaps, gorgeous and tactile blankets.

City Curtains
At the Red Lion Inn
Stockbridge, MA 01262
(800) 244-6040

Ready-made draperies, sophisticated but simple, in silk, damask, velvet (with pearls!), batiste, and linen; also hardware.

Country Curtains
(same as above)

Draperies with country charm, plus curtain hardware, from the same family-run firm.

Crate & Barrel
P.O. Box 9059
Wheeling, IL 60090-9059
(800) 323-5461

Furnishings, tableware, lighting, and accessories, all simple and classic.

Cuddledown of Maine
312 Canco Road
P.O. Box 1910
Portland, ME 04104-1910
(800) 323-6793

Linen-cotton "hotel" sheets, extra-long bedskirts and some classic beds.

Design Toscano
17 East Campbell Street
Arlington Heights, IL 60005
(800) 525-0733

Gargoyles, friezes, tapestries—everything for the baroque or Renaissance touch.

Eddie Bauer Home
Fifth & Union
P.O. Box 3700
Seattle, WA 98124-3700
(800) 426-8020

Lamps, beeswax candles, picture frames, bed linens.

Exposures
1 Memory Lane
P.O. Box 3615
Oshkosh, WI 54903-3615
(800) 222-4947 to order

Curio shelves, lamps, small cabinets, ledges and brackets, picture frames.

Flax Art & Design
P.O. Box 7216
San Francisco, CA 94120-7216
(800) 547-7778

Lamps, clocks, picture frames, and other decorative objects.

Gardeners Eden
Mail Order Department
P.O. Box 7307
San Francisco, CA 94120-7307
(800) 822-9600

Wicker and iron furniture, vases, plant stands, towel hooks—all with a garden theme.

Garnet Hill
Box 262 Main Street
Franconia, NH 03580
(800) 622-6216

Fine linens, towels, and curtain panels; handsome beds; the occasional piece of Herman Miller furniture.

Gump's Interiors by Mail
30 Maiden Lane
San Francisco, CA 94108
(800) 248-8677

Chairs, candlesticks, needlepoint pillows—a patrician-looking assortment. Ask for Gump's Interiors, not the regular Gump's catalog.

Historic Housefitters Co.
Farm to Market Road
Brewster, NY 10509
(800) 247-4111

Hand-forged, reproduction eighteenth-century hooks, hinges, hearth tools, and other hardware; reproduction period lighting.

Hold Everything
P.O. Box 7807
San Francisco, CA 94120
(800) 421-2264

Storage containers for clothing, CDs, files, cosmetics, books.

Home Decorators Collection
2025 Concourse Drive
St. Louis, MO 63146
(800) 245-2217

Amid the many first-apartment clichés, a few gems: clean-lined halogen lights, pedestals shaped like classical columns.

The Horchow Home Collection
The Horchow Fine Linen Collection
P.O. Box 620048
Dallas, TX 75262-0048
(800) 527-0303

Handsome and luxurious-looking furnishings and linens.

Janovic/Plaza's Incomplete Catalog for Decorative and Scenic Painters
30-35 Thomson Avenue
Long Island City, NY 11101
(718) 786-4444 in New York City; (800) 772-4381 outside

What on earth do they mean by incomplete? This immense catalog is crammed with Victorian-style embossed wallcoverings, tools for faux paint finishes, ceiling medallions, and much more. Cost: $4.95.

Laura Ashley Home Furnishings
telephone only: (800) 429-7678

Upholstered furniture, fabrics, wallpapers, bed and bath linens, lamps, accessories, pillows. Cost: $4.95 plus shipping.

A nice added service: Ask for the telephone number of the Laura Ashley store nearest you that employs a home stylist (the company's term for interior designer). You can then have a free phone consultation with the stylist to help choose or coordinate your purchases.

Levenger: Tools for Serious Readers
420 Commerce Drive
Delray Beach, FL 33445
(800) 544-0880

Lighting, small tables, desks, desk organizers, and bookshelves.

Linen & Lace
4 Lafayette Street
Washington, MO 63090
(800) 332-LACE

Drapery panels and table linens in many lace patterns.

Maine Cottage Furniture
P. O. Box 935
Yarmouth, ME 04096-1935
(207) 846-1430

Graceful wooden furniture, appealingly plain, in historic colors like cornflower and oxblood.

Martha By Mail
P.O. Box 60060
Tampa, FL 33630-0060
(800) 950-7130

A collection of Martha Stewart's home accessories, including soaps in the colors of her now-famous Araucana chicken eggs.

Museum of Modern Art
Mail Order Department
11 West 53rd Street
New York, NY 10019-5401
(800) 447-6662

Great modern design, from a pearwood tissue box to a simple CD rack.

Neiman Marcus at Home
Neiman Marcus Pink Sale
P.O. Box 650589
Dallas, TX 75265-0589
(800) 825-8000

Semiopulent home furnishings. Ask for both catalogs by name; they have separate mailing lists.

Pearl Paint Company
308 Canal Street
New York, NY 10013-2572
800-451-PEARL

Tabourets—those handy, rolling stacks of drawers and pull-out trays—are discounted here. Everything else is for artists.

Peterman's Eye
The J. Peterman Company
1318 Russell Cave Road
Lexington, Kentucky 40505
(800) 231-7341

An exotic (and quirky) selection of home furnishings and accessories.

Plummer-McCutcheon
Operations Center
9180 Le Saint Drive
Fairfield, OH 45014
(800) 321-1484

Mostly clothing, but a few intriguing accent pieces for the home.

Pottery Barn
P.O. Box 7044
San Francisco, CA 94120
(800) 922-5507

From sofas, sisal, and silverware to a collection of classics.

Renovator's
P.O. Box 2515
Conway, NH 03818-2515
(800) 659-2211

Pedestal sinks, embossed English wallpapers and borders, plaster-look Victorian ceiling medallions.

Rue de France
78 Thames Street
Newport, RI 02840
(800) 777-0998

Drapery panels, fabric "shutters" and pillows, in lace designs and French provincial patterns.

Saks Fifth Avenue Folio:
Design for the Home
557 Tuckahoe Road
Yonkers, NY 10710
(800) 345-3454

Rugs, lighting, reproduction antique furniture and elegant accessories.

Sanctuary
(800) 726-2882

Cher launched this mail-order company, choosing objects with a rich gothic image—from gargoyles and candelabras to sofas and cabinetry. There's clothing, too, if you want to dress the part.

Shades of Light
5609F Patterson Avenue
Richmond, VA 23226
(800) 262-6612

Lamps of every imaginable description, including hanging lanterns, sconces, and chandeliers.

Shaker Workshop
P.O. Box 8001
Ashburnham, MA 01430
(800) 840-9121

Graceful Shaker-style furnishings, preassembled or in do-it-yourself kit form; also charming accessories (like miniature Shaker tables that turn out to be salt and pepper shakers).

Smith & Hawken
Two Arbor Lane, Box 6900
Florence, KY 41022-6900
(800) 776-3336

Spiky wreaths, plant stands, fireplace tools, vases, and planters.

Spiegel
P.O. Box 182563
Columbus, OH 43218
(800) 345-4500

Stylish and practical furniture and accessories; you could furnish the whole house from these pages. Cost: $10, though discount offers frequently appear in Spiegel's magazine ads.

Staples
111 Middlesex Turnpike
P.O. Box 450
Burlington, MA 01803
(800) 333-3330

Inexpensive halogen and standard lighting.

Sugar Hill
1037 Front Avenue
Columbus, GA 31902
(800) 344-6125

Painted furniture, lavish bed linens, headboards, accessories.

Tassel Time
1249 Stirling Road
Dania, FL 33004
(800) 294-6677

Tassels, trimmings, and tiebacks.

Van Dyke's Restorers
P.O. Box 278
Woonsocket, SD 57385
(800) 843-3320

Architectural embellishments; vintage-looking knobs and handles; reproduction antique lamps, old-fashioned oval frames with convex glass—it may be all in black and white, but it makes great reading.

Windoware
Smith & Noble
P.O. Box 1838
Corona, CA 91718
(800) 248-8888

Custom-fitted blinds by mail order, in standard wood, bamboo, metal, and fabric; also valances made of handsome woodwork. Custom blinds are not returnable (unless flawed), so remember the carpenter's maxim: Measure twice, cut once.

STENCILING CATALOGS

These catalogs feature artistic and architectural designs, not the ducks-and-daisies motifs of the past.

Dressler Stencil Company
11030 173rd Avenue S.E.
Renton, WA 98059
(206) 226-0306

Stencils include eagle feathers, a spiraling topiary, and an understated grapevine designed to wander randomly across a wall. Cost: $5.

Helen Foster Stencils
71 Main Street
Sanford, ME 04073
(207) 490-2625

These Arts and Crafts motifs are stylized designs based on nature; there's a frieze of ginkgo leaves, one of seahorses, another of oak leaves. Cost: $5

The Stencil Collector
1723 Tilghman Street
Allentown, PA 18104
(610) 433-2105

Ask for Catalog II, which has grand English architectural stencils: pillars, columns, arches, balustrades, urns, bamboo. Cost: $5. (Catalog I contains more ornamental designs and is also $5.)

V. & Olga Decorating Company
159 Beach 123rd Street
Rockaway Park, NY 11694
(718) 634-4415

Classic architectural ornaments: moldings, borders, ceiling medallions, rosettes, urns and damask patterns, designed to create a three-dimensional effect suggestive of plasterwork. Cost: $5.